Total Quality Management in Human Service Organizations

SAGE HUMAN SERVICES GUIDES

A series of books edited by ARMAND LAUFFER and CHARLES D. GARVIN. Published in cooperation with the University of Michigan School of Social Work and other organizations.

Total Quality Management in Human Service Organizations

Lawrence L. Martin

SHSG SAGE HUMAN SERVICES GUIDE 67

Published in cooperation with the University of Michigan School of Social Work

SAGE Publications
International Educational and Professional Publisher
Newbury Park   London   New Delhi

For information address:

 SAGE publications, Inc.
2455 Teller Road
Newbury Park, California 91320
E-mail: order@sagepub.com

SAGE publications Ltd.
6 Bonhill Street
London EC2A 4PU
United Kingdom

SAGE Publications India Pvt. Ltd.
M-32 Market
Greater Kailash I
New Delhi 110 048 India

Printed in the United States of America

Library of Congress Cataloging-in-Publication Data

Martin, Lawrence L.
    Total quality management in human service organizations / Lawrence
L. Martin.
        p. cm.—(Sage human services guides; vol. 67)
    "Published in cooperation with the University of Michigan School
of Social Work."
    Includes bibliographical references.
    ISBN 0-8039-4949-9 (cl.).—ISBN 0-8039-4950-2 (pbk.)
    1. Human services—United States—Management.   2. Total quality
management—United States.   I. Title.   II. Series: Sage human
services guides; v. 67.
    HV95.M2743   1993
    361'.0068'5—dc20   93-2580
                                                            CIP

96 97 98 99 00 01 10 9 8 7 6 5 4 3

Sage Production Editor: Yvonne Könneker

CONTENTS

PREFACE

The impetus for this book was the realization that the human services have largely ignored the total quality management (TQM) movement. While both business and government as well as the health services have embraced TQM, one finds little mention of this new managerial wave in the human services literature. I hope this book will help spread the word about TQM among human service professionals.

The purpose of this book is to provide the reader with an overview of what TQM is all about. The book stresses the point that TQM is a new philosophy of management and is not simply a new set of tools that human service managers can pick and choose from. I have also tried to point out what I believe is a basic compatibility between the underlying values of TQM and those of the human services in general and social work in particular.

I owe a debt of gratitude to several individuals for their assistance in making this book a reality. I want to thank Steve McLaughlin, Arlene Sarver, Linda Mushkatel, and Pat Matthews, who provided me with information and insights into the TQM programs of the Maricopa County Department of Social Services. I also want to thank Marquita Flemming and Dale Grenfell of Sage Publications. Finally, a special thanks goes to Armand Lauffer, who saw the value in this book and helped guide its preparation.

LAWRENCE L. MARTIN
Boca Raton, Florida
March 1993

Chapter 1

QUALITY MANAGEMENT
The New Managerial Wave

Thousands of businesses and government agencies across the country are learning how to provide higher quality products and services while simultaneously increasing productivity and reducing costs. If there is a secret behind their success, it is one that is increasingly being shared openly. The secret is quality management. When quality becomes an organizational goal, problems of performance are recast under a different light that illuminates new options. If quality management can work for business and government, there is no reason why it should not work for human service organizations.

Some human service professionals may be inclined to think that quality management, what is also referred to as TQM (total quality management), is just another managerial wave that will sweep across the organizational landscape today and be gone tomorrow. Such suspicions are well founded. Since the 1960s each successive decade has seen the appearance of at least one new managerial wave that was supposed to be the solution to managing human service organizations. The 1960s saw the advent of program planning and budgeting (PPBS). Management by objectives (MBO) appeared on the scene in the early 1970s, followed in the latter part of the decade by zero-base budgeting (ZBB) and quality circles (QC). During the 1980s the search for excellence and privatization were touted as solutions to the problems of human service organizations. While vestiges of these past managerial waves are still to be found in many human service organizations today, most never lived up to their advance billings.

So what is new about quality management, and why should human service administrators get excited about yet another managerial wave? There are at least four good reasons. First, the human services are experiencing a quality crisis that is eroding client, citizen, and contributor confidence. Second, quality products and services create loyal customers, which is the answer to winning back the confidence of these same groups. Third, quality is free. Fourth, quality management—unlike most past managerial waves—is compatible with traditional human service and social work values.

THE QUALITY CRISIS IN THE HUMAN SERVICES

Support for the human services in general, and government-provided and -funded human services in particular, is at an all-time low. The federal government, as well as the 50 states, is grappling with paralyzing budget deficits. The solution of choice appears to be dramatic reductions—and in some instances curtailment—of funding for human services. For example, in fiscal year 1991 Massachusetts and California, historically two of the more progressive and compassionate states of the union, slashed funding for human services by $1 billion and $700 million, respectively (Kettner & Martin, 1993, p. 1). Even when good economic times return, it will take human service organizations years to make up the lost financial ground; some may never totally recover. The damage being done to people and families in the interim is incalculable.

A question that has not been fully explored is, why the sudden dramatic erosion of support for the human services? True, the human services have never enjoyed overwhelming citizen and taxpayer support, but the level of disapproval today suggests something more than just a general antipathy. Evidence suggests that this loss of support can be attributed to a perception that human service organizations provide poor quality products and services. In the final analysis, some of the criticism may be valid. Not all human service programs work as well as they should, and the general public may be telling us to shape up. Consider the following:

- A majority of citizens believe that government at all levels is simply not operating competently. The citizen *disapproval rate* is greatest for the federal government (69%), but is only marginally better for state governments (60%) and local governments (56%) (Carr & Littman, 1990, p. 9).
- Only a slim majority (54%) of citizens are satisfied with the overall quality of government services (Carr & Littman, 1990, p. 9).

- An analysis of citizen satisfaction surveys in 63 local governments nation-wide found that only 54% of the general public is satisfied with the operation of human services programs. The approval rate is somewhat higher (69.4%) for services to the elderly, but even this figure still means that more than 30% of citizens are generally dissatisfied with human service programs (Miller & Miller, 1991, p. 183).

Social scientists like Seymour Martin Lipset and William Schneider suggest that the declining satisfaction with government, including govern-ment human services, is based on the issue of performance and is not a challenge to the basic worth of government or government human services (cited in Kettle, 1988, p. 2). The issue then is not the need for, or the benefit of, government human services that is being questioned but rather the quality and performance of government human service organizations.

These findings might also be extended to private sector human service organizations. Most government human services today are ac-tually provided by private sector organizations through purchase of service contracts (Saidel, 1991; Salamon, 1987; Terrell, 1987). It is not unusual for many private sector human service organizations to derive upwards of 60% of their total revenues from government contracts (Terrell, 1987).

Private sector human service organizations also have their own qual-ity image problems. Not even the most prestigious appear exempt. For example, the American Red Cross is still trying to recover from a series of blows to its quality image brought about by problems with its blood program and the handling of disaster contributions (*Newsweek*, 1992). The United Way of America has also suffered a serious blow to its quality image, as a result of the $500,000 annual compensation pro-vided to its former CEO (*Time*, 1992).

Public dissatisfaction, however, is not based on scandal alone. It is often the result of overblown rhetoric by the supporters of human service programs, or by the refusal of human service organizations to address valid concerns raised by the general public. This latter point is evident when we examine recent experiences in the business sector.

The American automobile industry chose to ignore, misread, or dismiss the concerns and complaints of its customers. Those same customers started buying Japanese cars because Toyota, Honda, and Nissan listened. Detroit simply failed to understand the implications of the customer multiplier effect (Peters & Austin, 1985, p. 104). Both satisfied and dissatisfied customers tell others about their experiences. Dissatisfied customers, however, tend to relate their expe-riences to more people. According to one study, dissatisfied customers, on average, tell 9 or 10 other people about their experiences (Carr & Littman, 1990, p. 33).

What are the implications of the customer multiplier effect for human service organizations? If even 90% of customers are satisfied with the quality of a human service organization's products and services, 10% still are not. When this 10% is multiplied by a factor of 10, the organizational implications of dissatisfied customers take on a whole different perspective. The problem for most human service organizations is that they have no idea whether their customers are satisfied or dissatisfied because they have never bothered to find out.

The customer multiplier effect lies at the heart of many of the problems being experienced by human service organizations today. Despite the fact that the human services in general, and social work in particular, have always maintained that the client comes first, we have historically done a rather poor job of treating clients as customers. Clients have things done *to* them; customers have things done *for* them. Just as the multiplier effect of dissatisfied customers eventually overwhelmed Detroit, the multiplier effect of dissatisfied customers threatens to overwhelm both the public and private human services. The solution to this problem is for human service organizations to redirect their efforts to the pursuit of quality products and services.

Is the problem with quality in human service organizations being overstated? Those who think so should consider the current situation of the Florida Department of Health and Rehabilitative Services (FHRS), the state's omnibus health and human services agency. The perception of customers is that FHRS provides low-quality and ineffective services. The customer multiplier effect has finally overtaken the organization. Even before the devastation caused by Hurricane Andrew, Florida's Governor Lawton Chiles initiated a massive restructuring of FHRS, with the goal of forcing the department to become more responsive to customer preferences. If the restructuring fails to restore customer confidence, the department may well be dismantled, and its programs and functions assigned to existing or new state departments or transferred to county governments.

QUALITY CREATES LOYAL CUSTOMERS

Quality management programs create loyal customers. The notion of the loyal customer has a great deal of significance for human service organizations. Customers who believe their human service organizations are delivering quality products and services will continue to support those organizations through thick and thin. This support can take the form of volunteering time, contributing money, and perhaps most important, lending political support to the organization as it competes for scarce resources with other agencies and with other societal needs.

The notion of loyal customers as a political resource is particularly relevant for human service organizations today. At a macro level, the human services are in competition with other societal needs, such as education, health care, infrastructure maintenance, and others. At a micro level, human service organizations are in competition with one another for limited public and private funds. The perception of the quality of the human services in general may well determine its allocation of future national resources vis-à-vis other competing societal needs. Likewise, the perception of the product and service quality of individual human service organizations may well determine their allocation of future human service resources. In both instances, the key to future survival is the support of loyal customers.

QUALITY IS FREE

A particularly attractive feature of quality management programs is that *quality is free*. A substantial body of research now exists, demonstrating that the costs of implementing quality management programs are recouped by greater productivity and lower total product and service costs (Crosby, 1980; Dobyns & Crawford-Mason, 1991; Feigenbaum, 1983; Zeithaml, Parasuraman, & Berry, 1990). Put another way, the cost of producing high-quality products and services is zero, while the cost of producing low-quality products and services is equal to the cost of putting things right and dealing with disgruntled customers.

The notion that quality actually improves productivity is somewhat revolutionary and runs counter to long-held American notions about productivity and productivity improvement. The traditional American conceptualization of productivity is the ratio of inputs to outputs (see Figure 1.1). This input/output relationship is the classic industrial engineering definition of efficiency. For example, take the case of two intake workers (W1 and W2), employed by the same human services organization, performing the same job tasks, and being paid the same wage. W1 is able to process an average of six applications per hour, while W2 processes an average of five. According to the traditional American view of productivity, W1 is more productive than W2.

Quality management, however, maintains that the singular pursuit of productivity through a focus on efficiency is self-defeating. Quality

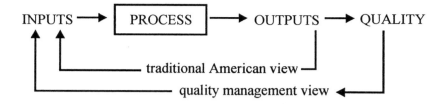

Figure 1.1. The Traditional American and the Quality Management Views of Productivity

management experts would say that any human service organization that strives to increase productivity by increasing efficiency must inevitably wind up sacrificing quality. Decreased quality necessarily leads to lower productivity and higher-cost products and services. Low-quality products and services have more defects and generate more customer complaints, which, in turn, require additional resources to correct. Referring again to Figure 1.1, quality management theory includes quality as the ultimate measure of productivity. Because high-quality products and services have fewer defects and generate fewer customer complaints, productivity is actually enhanced when an organization focuses on quality. In the case of the two intake workers, if W1 makes an average 1.2 incorrect eligibility determinations per hour while W2 makes none, W2 is the more productive. The organization will have to expend additional resources correcting the mistakes of W1 and dealing with unhappy customers.

Does it really cost a lot of money to correct mistakes? Informed judgment as well as empirical evidence suggests that it does:

- Phil Crosby (1992, p. 36) estimates that the cost of not doing things right the first time for a typical service organization is equal to around 40% of total operating costs.
- J. M. Juran (1989, p. 199) estimates that for the whole decade of the 1980s, about one-third of all the work performed by all American companies was actually rework because of quality problems.
- In the early 1980s Merrill Lynch & Company estimated that the cost of correcting mistakes and placating dissatisfied customers was costing more than $200 million a year (Zeithaml et al., 1990, p. 11).
- More recently, the Hewlett Packard Company discovered that rework and dealing with customer complaints cost the company 20% of revenues and involved the time and effort of 25% of company employees (Sheer, 1991, p. 24).

As these estimates indicate, the costs of not providing quality products and services can be so great that the costs of implementing quality management programs are usually recovered.

QUALITY MANAGEMENT
AND HUMAN SERVICE VALUES

A unique advantage of quality management is its basic compatibility with human service and social work values. Any managerial system that does not preach the maximization of efficiency should be inherently appealing to most human service professionals. The human services have long objected to the primacy generally afforded efficiency by most management systems (Pruger & Miller, 1991a, 1991b).

Quality management also strongly emphasizes the use of customer feedback in attempting to constantly improve the quality of products and services. In many respects this aspect of quality management is reflective of the maxim that the needs of clients should be put first. Quality management also stresses the self-worth of employees, cooperation between employees, team building, and a partnership relationship between public and private sector human service organizations. Finally, quality management stresses prevention over remediation. Human service organizations have long stressed prevention over remediation as a preferred strategy, although prevention has been hard to sell to most public and private funding sources. Quality management provides theoretical as well as empirical support for preferring prevention over remediation. A basic tenet of quality management is that it is cheaper in the long run to build quality into an organization's products and services (prevention) than it is to expend additional resources on rework and dissatisfied customers (remediation).

IS YOUR ORGANIZATION READY
FOR QUALITY MANAGEMENT?

Quality management takes a unique perspective on customers, organizations, and the roles of management, employees, and contractors. Some human service organizations may find that quality management requires a dramatic rethinking and reordering of the managerial and administrative precepts that have guided them over the years; others may find that little change in thinking is required. The exercise in Box 1.1 is designed to assess a human service organization's basic readiness

BOX 1.1 Quality Management Readiness Test

Check whether each of the following statements is generally reflective of how your organization goes about its business:

1. In my organization, we continually tinker with and fine-tune the quality of all our products and services, even when things appear to be working well.
   Yes _____ No _____

2. In my organization, clients, families, stakeholders, and other customers are active participants in determining how best to improve the quality of our products and services.
   Yes _____ No _____

3. In my organization, cooperation between departmental units is prized more highly than is competition.
   Yes _____ No _____

4. In my organization, managers and staff persons usually gather and analyze data on a perceived problem before actually making any changes in the way we provide our products and services.
   Yes _____ No _____

5. In my organization, we have an ongoing training program so that managers and staff can learn how to do their jobs better.
   Yes _____ No _____

6. In my organization, the flow of communication is top-down, down-up, and sideways. Everybody talks to, and shares information with, everyone else.
   Yes _____ No _____

7. In my organization, managers and supervisors are looked on as consultants who are there to ensure that staff succeed at their jobs.
   Yes _____ No _____

8. In my organization, we place an emphasis on teams and teamwork rather than on individual effort.
   Yes _____ No _____

9. In my organization, our contractors are treated as partners, and we work cooperatively with them to provide the highest quality products and services possible.
   Yes _____ No _____

for quality management. The exercise involves responding either "yes" or "no" to a series of nine propositions. After taking the test, the exercise can be self-scored.

All nine propositions are generally reflective of quality management practices. Consequently, the more statements that the reader agrees with, the less the amount of change that should be required for your organization to adopt quality management. As a rule of thumb, the following self-scoring system is suggested:

Number of Statements Checked "Yes"	Amount of Change Required
7–9	Minor
4–6	Moderate
0–3	Major

The Quality Management Readiness Test provides a sort of sneak preview of what quality management is all about. In subsequent chapters each of the concepts hinted at in the test will be dealt with at length. The following two chapters deal with the history and philosophy of quality management. Some readers may consider jumping over these chapters to get directly to the so-called meat, or tools, of quality management. This approach is not recommended. Quality management is a philosophy of management. Those quality management programs that fail, generally do so because managers attempt to jump over the philosophy and get right to the tools. For quality management to be successful, an organization must adopt not only the tools but also the management philosophy that enables the tools to work as intended.

A lot of what will be presented in this book may be new and different to some readers. Long-cherished beliefs as to the best ways to manage a human service organization will be questioned. The reader is invited to remain skeptical throughout the discussion but is asked to withhold final judgment until all the material has been presented.

Chapter 2

WHAT IS TOTAL QUALITY MANAGEMENT (TQM)?

Many Americans tend to equate quality management with Japanese management because Japan was the first country to totally embrace the notion. The Japanese did innovate in this area, but so did a number of Americans, foremost among them being W. Edwards Deming, Phil Crosby, J. M. Juran, and Armand Feigenbaum. Each of these major American quality experts approaches quality management from a slightly different perspective and advocates a slightly different system. To differentiate American quality management systems from Japanese quality management systems and to integrate the theories and writings of the major American quality experts, the term *total quality management* (TQM) was coined. TQM has become a sort of umbrella term, used to describe various American quality management systems operating in both the public and private sectors.

TQM has been defined as "the application of quantitative methods and human resources to improve the material and services supplied to an organization, all the processes within an organization, and the degree to which the needs of the customer are met, now and in the future" (Mossard, 1991, p. 223). The reference to both quantitative methods and human resources in this definition is reflective of TQM's attempt to integrate the analytical perspective of scientific management with the human relations school's focus on organizations, groups, and employees (Kronenberg & Loeffler, 1991).

Scientific management, sometimes referred to as Taylorism (Taylor, 1919), sought ways to increase productivity by applying the scientific method to the study of workers' jobs. Taylor and his disciples advocated detailed planning and analysis of work processes to find the best ways to perform job functions (Lerner & Wanat, 1992, p. 65). Some contemporary critics suggest that scientific management sought to fit the employee to the job. However, according to Peter Drucker (1991), scientific management has suffered from a "bad rap" over the years. What scientific management actually attempted to do, according to Drucker, was teach employees how to work *smarter* rather than *harder*. Today, working smarter, not harder, is considered the essence of productivity improvement (Brinkerhoff & Dressler, 1990, p. 20). As a management doctrine, scientific management had several major drawbacks, including the lack of employee involvement in decision making about their jobs. Because employees were treated as cogs in a wheel, scientific management was rightly criticized as being depersonalizing and dehumanizing.

At the opposite end of the spectrum from scientific management stands the human relations school (e.g., Barnard, 1938; Maslow, 1962; Mayo, 1945). The focus of the human relations school is on people. Proponents of the human relations school study teams, groups, and organizations and are concerned with such issues as organizational culture, formal and informal group structures and communication, and attempting to make the nature of work more compatible with the human condition (Kronenberg & Loeffler, 1991, p. 210). In short, the human relations school seeks ways to fit the job to the employee. The human relations school has predominated over the past 50 years, while scientific management has generally been dismissed as a passé managerial doctrine.

TQM attempts to blend the analytical and working smarter aspects of scientific management with the organizational, group, and employee focus of the human relations school. Until recently such an effort would have been scorned. But TQM has succeeded in demonstrating the feasibility of melding the positive aspects of these two diverse management doctrines, while mitigating the negative aspects of scientific management. For example, a basic tenet of TQM is that only through systematic analysis can a real understanding of quality problems be achieved (Gabor, 1990; Gitlow, Gitlow, Oppenheim, & Oppenheim, 1989). This analytical perspective is reflective of the scientific management tradition. A concept frequently associated with TQM is the notion of "zero-defects" (Crosby, 1980). Zero-defects is the idea that the ultimate goal of a TQM system should be the reduction of variation in the production of products and services to absolute zero. Zero-defects is the modern day systems' equivalent to the old scientific management objective of trying to find the best way to perform job functions so as to minimize errors.

Some human service professionals may find the notion of zero-defects a bit alien. Visions are conjured up of workers huddled around an assembly line, attempting to produce the perfect widget. This vision seems rather distant, if not downright antithetical, to concerns about client processing. It must be remembered, however, that Crosby—as well as the other major American quality management experts—are products of a business environment. We should not let this background prejudice our thinking. Instead, we should attempt to look beyond their choice of words in an effort to discover the real meaning behind them. When this approach is taken, we find that the concept of zero-defects has relevance for virtually all aspects of human endeavor, including the human services. Zero-defects simply means that any process can be improved on. Being good at something may still not be good enough. Let us assume that our society was to establish a quality standard for all human endeavor, not at zero-defects, but at the rate of one allowable error for every 1,000 attempts (a 99.9% average quality level). Would this level be good enough? Even with this stringent quality standard, our society would still experience

- 2,000 lost pieces of mail every hour.
- unsafe drinking water in every home and office for one hour each month.
- two short or long landings at our nation's airports every day.
- 15,000 newborn babies accidentally dropped in hospitals each year.
- 500 incorrect surgical operations each week.
- 1,500 incorrect prescriptions given out each month. (Mesa Community College, undated, p. 5)

Applied to the human services, a 99.9% average quality rate would still mean that one out of every 1,000 clients seen would be incorrectly denied Medicaid, food stamps, AFDC, and general assistance at every social services office in every city in every state, every single working day. When we look beyond the numbers and remember that each number represents a client with a problem, the only acceptable error rate is zero-defects.

Another basic tenet of TQM is the recognition that only through the management of people working in teams, groups, and organizations can the quality of products and services be improved (Carr & Littman, 1990; Goldense, 1991; Power, 1991). As one TQM expert (Feigenbaum, 1983, p. 6) has noted, "In the final analysis it is a pair of human hands which perform the important operations affecting product quality." This is Feigenbaum's way of saying that process is important. The way people perform their jobs largely determines the quality of products and services. In human service terms, Feigenbaum's hands metaphor can be taken to mean that client processing is important and is a critical aspect of product and service quality. This recognition of the important role played by individual employees in an organization is reflective of the human relations school.

The emphasis on blending aspects of both scientific management and the human relations school points out a major difference between TQM and past managerial waves. TQM is first and foremost a philosophy of management.

A BRIEF HISTORY OF TQM

TQM is based on the ideas and writings of four principal individuals: Deming (1982, 1986, 1990), Crosby (1980, 1985, 1992), Juran (1988, 1989), and Feigenbaum (1983). Deming and Juran are clearly the patriarchs of not only TQM but also the whole quality movement. Both men have been speaking and writing about quality for some 50 years. It is W. Edwards Deming, however, who is arguably the most influential of all the quality experts and the man who has come to symbolize quality management in both Japan and the United States. Studies demonstrate that the majority of TQM programs are based at least in part on Deming's approach to quality management (Krone, 1991, p. 196). Any discussion of quality, quality management, or TQM must necessarily make some special mention of W. Edwards Deming.

W. EDWARDS DEMING

Deming is a statistician. He developed his notions of quality management and statistical quality control during the 1920s while working at Western Electric's Hawthorn plant in Chicago. This is the same plant where the famous "Hawthorn studies" were conducted. Later Deming moved to the Massachusetts Institute of Technology (MIT), where he lectured, wrote, and talked about quality. Deming's ideas were largely ignored in the United States. After World War II, the Japanese government invited Deming—along with J. M. Juran—to lecture to Japanese business and government leaders on the concept of quality management and statistical quality control. Statistical quality control refers to the use of statistics to reduce variation in processes and thus to improve the quality of products and services.

The idea of quality management caught on and flourished in Japan and is considered to be part of the explanation for Japan's economic prowess today. *Kaizen,* the Japanese term for quality management, is based to a great extent on Deming's ideas (Imai, 1986). In Japan, Deming is regarded as something of a national hero. The highest Japanese award for quality is called the "Deming Prize" in his honor. Deming and the concept of quality management only came to prominence in the United States in the early 1980s.

Deming's philosophy of quality management evolved over many years and it was not until late in his life that they found their full expression. In his major work, *Out of the Crisis* (1986), Deming sets down his philosophy of quality management in what has become known as his "14 points" (Table 2.1). Deming's 14 points can be reduced to a smaller number of fundamental concepts: constancy of purpose, continuous improvement, an understanding of variation, and profound knowledge (Dobyns & Crawford-Mason, 1991; Gabor, 1990). Constancy of purpose means understanding the nature of one's market and that a market has no end state, but is always changing and evolving. Continuous improvement means that there is no final or end state to quality; quality is always in a state of becoming. Continuous improvement enables an organization to hit the moving target of constancy of purpose. Variation refers to the deviations from standards that are present in the production of any product or the provision of any service. Quality improvement for Deming is based on understanding and reducing variation in systems and major processes. Profound knowledge is what Deming says is needed to implement his 14 points. Profound knowledge has four components: a systems perspective, an understanding of processes and variation, a theory of knowledge, and a knowledge of psychology in order to motivate people (Dobyns & Crawford-Mason, 1991, p. 59).

Deming teaches us that TQM is based on a philosophy of management that is quite different from traditional American notions and practices. From Deming we also learn about the importance of understanding and reducing variation in processes, that is, that the key to product and service quality in the human services lies in controlling the processes by which customers are served. Finally, we also learn from Deming that we cannot adopt the tools of TQM without adopting the philosophy of TQM. To attempt to do so is a prescription for failure.

PHIL CROSBY

Phil Crosby is concerned with the tools of TQM. Some say he stands at the polar opposite to Deming. Deming is frequently described as a TQM philosopher; Crosby is often described as a TQM technician.

Phil Crosby got his quality management start at the International Telephone and Telegraph Company (ITT). He left ITT after the success of his book *Quality Is Free* (Crosby, 1980). Crosby attempts to distill

TABLE 2.1 Deming's 14 Points

1. Create consistency of purpose toward improvement of product and service.
2. Awaken to the challenges of the new economic age and adopt a new philosophy.
3. Cease dependency on inspection to achieve quality.
4. Stop awarding business on the basis of price.
5. Constantly improve the system of production and service.
6. Institute training on the job.
7. Institute leadership.
8. Drive out fear.
9. Break down barriers between departments.
10. Eliminate slogans, exhortations, and targets aimed at zero-defects and new levels of productivity.
11. Eliminate quotas on the factory floor.
12. Remove barriers that rob people of the right to pride of workmanship.
13. Institute a vigorous program of education and self-improvement.
14. Put everybody in the company to work on accomplishing the transformation.

SOURCE: Deming (1986, pp. 23-24).

the philosophy and concepts of quality management down to simple ideas and tools that working managers in the public and private sectors can understand and relate to. Crosby, like Deming, has reduced his quality management approach down to 14 points (see Table 2.2). A comparison of Crosby's 14 points with those of Deming demonstrate Crosby's more technical orientation. Crosby's 14 points are actually a how-to TQM implementation strategy that begins with management commitment to quality (Point 1) and ends with "do it all over again" (Point 14), which is Crosby's way of saying that the pursuit of quality is never ending.

From Crosby we develop our understanding of zero-defects and the importance of "doing things right the first time." For the human services, Crosby's slogans can be taken to mean that excellence should be the standard that we all aspire to, rather than some utopian dream. Crosby also teaches us that while philosophy is important in TQM, successful implementation of a TQM program in a human service organization requires a great deal more than "a single gulp of philosophy" (Crosby, 1980, p. 13). Successful TQM programs require a great deal of personal and organizational effort.

TABLE 2.2 Crosby's 14 Points

---

1. Management Commitment
2. Quality Improvement Teams
3. Measurement
4. Cost of Quality
5. Quality Awareness
6. Corrective Action
7. Zero-Defects Planning
8. Employee Education
9. Zero-Defects Day
10. Goal Setting
11. Error Cause Removal
12. Recognition
13. Quality Councils
14. Do It All Over Again

SOURCE: P. Crosby (1980, pp. 112-119).

J. M. JURAN

Between the extremes represented by Deming and Crosby, falls J. M. Juran. Juran, like Deming, started out at the Western Electric Hawthorn Plant in Chicago in the 1920s. He also lectured and consulted with the Japanese after World War II. Juran published his first major work, *Quality Control Handbook*, in 1954. Juran's approach to TQM is closer to Deming's than to Crosby's. Nevertheless, Juran and Deming diverge on several key points. In particular, Juran believes that managing for quality is similar to any other managerial framework and does not necessarily require a total organizational revolution. Juran teaches a threefold approach to TQM: quality planning, quality control, and quality improvement. Overall, Juran's approach to quality management is quite flexible. To Juran, statistical techniques, as well as a lot of the other trappings of TQM, are useful tools, nothing more (Juran, 1989).

Juran teaches us the importance of top management commitment to quality if a TQM program is to prove successful. From Juran we also learn the important role of quality councils in providing organizational focus and direction to TQM efforts (Juran, 1989, p. 43).

ARMAND FEIGENBAUM

The final member of the big four American TQM experts is Armand Feigenbaum. His classic work, *Total Quality Control*, first appeared in

1951 but was reissued in an expanded version as late as 1983, nearly 30 years later. Feigenbaum spent several years as the General Electric company's top quality expert, where he also came to believe that quality management is more than a tool for managers to use; it is rather a way of managing. Feigenbaum calls his approach "total quality control" (Feigenbaum, 1983).

From Feigenbaum we learn about the "cost of quality" and why it is cheaper in the long run to build quality into our products and services than to correct errors later. Feigenbaum is generally credited with being the first person to talk about the cost of quality (Dobyns & Crawford-Mason, 1991, p. 72).

TQM AND SERVICE ORGANIZATIONS

Deming, Crosby, Juran, and Feigenbaum all got their start and developed their quality management approaches while working in the manufacturing, or production, side of business. This ancestry frequently gives rise to concerns about the applicability of TQM to other types of organizational settings, including service industries, government agencies, and human service organizations. Deming (1986) is adamant that TQM is applicable to all service organizations, public sector as well as private sector. This sentiment is shared by both Juran (1989) and Crosby (1980). Juran refers to the application of TQM to manufacturing and production focused organizations as "little Q." The application of TQM to all types of organizations, including services, he calls "big Q" (Juran, 1989, p. 48).

Researchers studying service organizations point out that services possess certain characteristics that set them distinctly apart from products (e.g., Murdick, Render, & Russell, 1990). Table 2.3 highlights some of the more important characteristics of services.

An analysis of these service characteristics might well lead one to conclude that TQM is perhaps even more applicable to service organizations, including human service organizations, than it is to manufacturing organizations. For example, TQM focuses on customers, but so do service organizations, including human service organizations. For many human service organizations, customers (i.e., clients) are actually a part of the service delivery process, as is the case with counseling, both child and adult day care, foster care, and others. TQM also focuses on variation and process control, but so do service organizations, including human service organizations. Because service organizations produce nonstandard outputs, quality control is necessarily process control. In the human services, no two clients who complete a service

TABLE 2.3 Characteristics of Services

1. Services produce nontangible outputs.
2. Services produce nonstandard outputs.
3. Services involve high levels of customer contact.
4. Service quality control is primarily process control.

SOURCE: Adapted from Murdick et al. (1990, p. 27).

plan (an output) are ever likely to be exactly alike. Thus, human service organizations deal with nonstandard outputs, thereby requiring that service quality control become essentially process control. It is exactly these essential characteristics of service organizations, including human service organizations, that make them such good candidates for TQM programs.

Empirically, TQM has already been successfully applied in a number of public and private service organizations (Milakovich, 1990) including several applications in the health care area (Walton, 1990) and a limited number in the human services (Osborn & Gaebler, 1992).

THE TQM WAVE HITS THE UNITED STATES

The decade of the 1980s in the United States has been called a period of consciousness raising regarding quality (Albrecht, 1992, p. 2). The 1990s are projected to be the decade of TQM implementation (*Business Week*, 1991, p. 57). Such diverse American corporations as Corning, Ford, General Motors, Hospital Corporation of America, Motorola, Westinghouse, Xerox, and others have all initiated TQM programs over the last several years (FQI, 1991; Gabor, 1990; Walton, 1990). Today some 3,000 American companies have active TQM programs in place (Milakovich, 1990, p. 22).

In 1987 the federal government created the Malcolm Baldrige Quality Award. The award is named for a former Secretary of Commerce. The purpose of the Baldrige Award is similar to that of the Deming Award in Japan—to focus national attention on the pursuit of quality. Winners of the Baldrige Award include the Cadillac Division of General Motors, Federal Express, IBM, Motorola, and Xerox.

TQM is also expanding rapidly in the public sector. At the federal level, some 235 quality programs are in operation in such diverse federal departments and agencies as the Department of Defense, the Environmental Protection Agency, the Internal Revenue Service, NASA, and the Office of Personnel Management (Carr & Littman, 1990; Cohen & Brand, 1990; Milakovich, 1990; Mossard, 1991). The level of quality management activity in the federal government has become so significant that a Federal Quality Institute (FQI) now exists to provide leadership and coordinate the various programs (FQI, 1991). In 1989 the federal government created the President's Award for Quality. Modeled after the Baldrige Award, this award recognizes federal agencies and departments that demonstrate "exemplary quality improvements" (FQI, 1991, p. 25).

The TQM wave is also being felt at the state and local government levels. The states of Arkansas, Florida, Wisconsin, and Vermont have all launched notable statewide TQM programs, while the states of Arizona, California, Michigan, and Pennsylvania, among others, are experimenting with TQM on a department-by-department basis (*Business Week*, 1991; Carr & Littman, 1990; Milakovich, 1990; Osborn & Gaebler, 1992; Strong & Ford, 1992). At the local government level, a recent survey reports that some 50 major county and municipal governments nationwide are actively engaged in implementing TQM programs (Carr & Littman, 1990, p. 260).

When it comes to the implementation of TQM in human service organizations, there is a dearth of published information. Yet a few progressive human service organizations, like the Maricopa County Department of Social Services (MCDOSS) in Phoenix, Arizona, are moving forward with vigorous TQM programs. Some of the work in quality management being done by MCDOSS is featured in succeeding chapters.

Chapter 3

TQM AS A PHILOSOPHY OF MANAGEMENT

TQM is first and foremost a philosophy of management. This is what makes TQM different from previous managerial waves. Past managerial waves, like PPBS, MBO, and ZBB, were essentially tool-based systems. These tools could be adopted by a human service organization without any significant changes being made in its basic approach to management. TQM is different. Although TQM does employ a variety of tools, simply adopting the tools does not mean that a human service organization is practicing TQM. The observation has been made that it is impossible to develop a stand-alone TQM tools handbook because TQM is a philosophy of management that requires a transformation of organizational cultures (*Business Week*, 1991, p. 11).

What is meant by a philosophy of management? A philosophy can be defined as the most general beliefs, concepts, and attitudes of an individual or group. TQM is a distillation of the beliefs, concepts, and attitudes of a group of quality experts. Consequently, to understand TQM as a philosophy of management, the group's basic tenets must be identified and made explicit. Unfortunately, the basic tenets of TQM are not set down on a stone tablet. How then does one develop an understanding of TQM as a philosophy of management? There appears to be two basic ways. First, an analysis can be made of the Malcolm Baldrige Award criteria. The Baldrige Award criteria are said to be reflective of the emerging TQM philosophy (Garvin, 1991, p. 82).

Second, an analysis can be made of the common philosophical ground shared by the big four American quality experts: Deming, Crosby, Juran, and Feigenbaum.

THE BALDRIGE AWARD CRITERIA

Table 3.1 presents the Baldrige Award criteria and scoring system. The criteria have widely differing values. Each major category is assigned a score that serves to identify its relative weight, or importance, compared to the other categories.

Four major categories dominate the Baldrige Award scoring system. In order of importance, they are (a) customer focus and satisfaction, (b) quality and operational results, (c) human resource development and management, and (d) management of process quality. In order to win the Baldrige Award, nominees must score well in each of these four categories.

To score well on the category of customer focus and satisfaction, nominees must demonstrate an organizational commitment to customers and customer satisfaction, that organizational plans and decisions are driven by customer concerns, and that systems are in place to routinely assess customer satisfaction with the organization's products and services.

At this point, it should perhaps be noted that TQM takes a more expansive definition of customer than just the direct recipient of a product or service. TQM defines customer broadly enough to include those groups most human service organizations deal with, including clients, their families or guardians, funding sources, accreditation bodies, and other stakeholders. The subject of customers is dealt with at length in Chapter 4.

To score well on the category of quality and operational results, nominees must demonstrate that significant improvements have been made in the overall quality of their products and services. To score well on the category of human resource development and management, nominees must demonstrate employee involvement and empowerment in decision making, and a commitment on the organization's part to employee training and recognition. Finally, to score well on the category of the management of process quality, nominees must demonstrate that systems are in place to insure quality planning, implementation, and evaluation, and that contractors and suppliers are actively involved in the quality improvement program.

More than 75% of the 1,000 points possible in the Baldrige Award scoring system are accounted for by these four categories. Thus, these four categories can be said to broadly reflect the basic areas that TQM considers important as a philosophy of management.

TABLE 3.1 Baldrige Award Categories and Point Values

Criteria	Points
1. Leadership	100
2. Information and Analysis	70
3. Strategic Quality Planning	60
4. Human Resource Development and Utilization	150
5. Management of Process Quality	140
6. Quality and Operational Results	180
7. Customer Focus and Satisfaction	300
Total points	1,000

SOURCE: *Malcolm Baldrige National Quality Award—1992 Award Criteria* (1992). Washington, DC: U.S. Department of Commerce and the National Institute of Standards and Technology, p. 12.

The reader might find it an interesting exercise to compare the answers given on the quality management readiness test from Chapter 1 with these four criteria from the Baldrige Award. How well would your organization measure up?

COMMON GROUND AMONG
THE BIG FOUR TQM EXPERTS

Deming, Crosby, Juran, and Feigenbaum disagree with each other—frequently with considerable vigor—over exactly what TQM means as a philosophy of management. Despite their areas of disagreement, however, several key areas of general agreement do exist. These areas of common ground also provide useful insights into TQM as a philosophy of management.

A content analysis was performed on the writings of the big four American quality experts. The purpose was to identify those common threads that deal with TQM as a philosophy of management. Additionally, a content analysis was performed on seven recent works that are themselves attempts to synthesize the major philosophical tenets of TQM (Carr & Littman, 1990; Dobyns & Crawford-Mason, 1991; Gabor, 1990; Kronenberg & Loeffler, 1991; Milakovich, 1990; Swiss, 1992; Watson & Hopp, 1992).

From the two content analyses, six key elements of general agreement were identified that appear to be central to an understanding of

TQM as a philosophy of management. These six key elements (see Table 3.2) are (a) quality as a primary organizational goal, (b) quality being determined by an organization's customers, (c) customer satisfaction being the fuel that drives organizations, (d) the study and reduction of variation in processes, (e) change being continuous and accomplished by teams and teamwork, and (f) top management commitment to promoting a culture of quality, employee empowerment, and a long-term perspective. As can be seen, these six key elements complement and help to further define the four primary Baldrige Award categories. These six key areas then can be said to constitute the basic underlying philosophy of TQM.

Because the focus of this book is on TQM in human service organizations, an additional key element is included. This element deals with the inclusion of contractors in TQM programs. Deming is the most forceful of the major quality experts in advocating this position. Deming's rationale is the realization that organizations that are heavily reliant on contractors cannot control the quality of their products and services without the involvement and commitment of their contractors to TQM principles. The Department of Defense has found Deming's contention to be particularly true in its own efforts to implement TQM (Carr & Littman, 1990). Likewise, the General Accounting Office identifies contractor involvement as a key element in successful private sector TQM programs (Watson & Hopp, 1992). Contractor involvement is also mentioned as a subcategory, albeit a minor one, of the Baldrige Award criteria.

Due to the significant amount of purchase of service contracting occurring today (Saidel, 1991; Salamon, 1987; Terrell, 1987), many human service organizations are heavily dependent on contractors for the quality of the products and services they provide. Consequently, the success of TQM in such organizations is dependent on the active participation of contractors.

DOES PHILOSOPHY REALLY MATTER?

How much difference does TQM as a philosophy of management really make? Do philosophical differences between what can be called the traditional American philosophy of management and TQM actually result in differences in style and substance?

Table 3.3 compares principles derived from traditional American management philosophy with TQM philosophical principles. Some of the major principles of traditional American management philosophy are (a) profits and bottom line considerations as the primary driving force, (b) a preference for competition over cooperation, (c) the belief

TABLE 3.2 Key Elements of TQM as a Philosophy of Management

1. Quality—is a primary organizational goal.
2. Customers—determine what quality is.
3. Customer Satisfaction—drives the organization.
4. Variation—in processes must be understood and reduced.
5. Change—is continuous and is accomplished by teams and teamwork.
6. Top Management Commitment—to promoting a culture of quality, employee empowerment, and a long-term perspective.

that change occurs in quantums, and (d) a penchant for what the Japanese call "cowboy management" (Imai, 1986), or entrepreneurial champions who battle bureaucracies to bring about innovation and change (Peters & Waterman, 1982). Finally, the slogan that may best characterize traditional American management philosophy is, "If it ain't broke, don't fix it." Underlying this slogan is the belief that when an organization is running smoothly, managers and employees can simply sit back and rest on their laurels.

TQM as a philosophy of management sees the world differently. TQM management principles include (a) quality as the force that drives organizations, (b) a preference for cooperation over competition, (c) the belief that change occurs continuously and gradually, and (d) a preference for teamwork over individualism. Finally, the slogan that may best capture TQM as a philosophy of management is, "Unattended systems tend to run down." This slogan refers to TQM's view that quality problems are due to too much variation occurring in an organization's major systems and processes. Quality is achieved by constantly tinkering with and fine-tuning an organization's major systems and processes in a never ending quest for improvement.

Do these philosophical differences actually translate into differing results? The General Accounting Office (GAO), the watchdog arm of Congress, sought an answer to this question back in the early 1990s. GAO discovered that only case study and anecdotal evidence existed at the time to support the contention that TQM actually worked. GAO decided to conduct the first ever comprehensive evaluation of TQM, by reviewing 20 American private sector businesses engaged in TQM programs. The GAO study revealed that on average the companies experienced a 10.3% overall reduction in defects and an 11.6% reduction in customer complaints (Watson & Hopp, 1992, p. 35).

TABLE 3.3 A Comparison of Traditional American Management Principles With TQM Management Principles

Traditional American Management Principles	Total Quality Management (TQM) Management Principles
The organization has multiple competing goals.	Quality is the primary organizational goal.
Financial concerns drive the organization.	Customer satisfaction drives the organization.
Management and professionals determine what quality is.	Customers determine what quality is.
The focus is on the status quo—"If it ain't broke, don't fix it."	The focus is on continuous improvement—"Unattended systems tend to run down."
Change is abrupt and is accomplished by champions battling the bureaucracy.	Change is continuous and is accomplished by teamwork.
Employees and departments compete with each other.	Employees and departments cooperate with each other.
Decisions are based on "gut feelings." It is better to do something than to do nothing.	Decisions are based on data and analysis. It is better to do nothing than to do the wrong thing.
Employee training is considered a luxury and a cost.	Employee training is considered essential and an investment.
Organizational communication is primarily top-down.	Organizational communication is top-down, down-up, and sideways.
Contractors are encouraged to compete with each other on the basis of price.	Long-term relationships are developed with contractors who deliver quality products and services.

SOURCE: Adapted from FQI (1991, pp. 15-17).

TQM as a philosophy of management is quite different from traditional American management philosophy. Some of the differences are of a macro nature, some are more micro, but all entail a different way of looking at organizations, change, and management/employee relations. In following chapters the implications of TQM as a philosophy of management will become even clearer as various aspects are explored in more depth.

Chapter 4

QUALITY AS AN ORGANIZATIONAL GOAL

Not long ago I was asked to review the monitoring practices of a government health and human service organization that had an extensive purchase of a service contracting program for nursing home services. The agency director said he was having quality problems with some of his contract facilities. In reading over several contract monitoring reports, I was surprised to find that different monitors could visit the same facility a few days apart and come away with totally different opinions as to the quality of the services being provided.

After a little exploration, I discovered something interesting. The organization used two different types of monitors, registered nurses (RNs) and social workers (MSWs). When the RNs monitored a facility, their perceptions of service quality appeared to be formed largely on the basis of medical considerations. Were patients' medical charts up-to-date? Had a physician seen each patient recently? Were the patients' medications being properly administered? When the MSWs monitored the same facility, their perceptions of service quality appeared to be formed largely on the basis of psychosocial factors. Were clients up and out of bed? Were clients responsive and interacting with others? Were client activities scheduled on a daily basis? How well did staff relate to clients?

The choice of terms used in the monitoring reports (patient versus client) was also interesting. The use of these contrasting terms suggested that at least two different professional perspectives were being used to assess quality. The quality problem actually being experienced here was that the government health and human service organization really had no definition of quality. Consequently, monitors simply used their own professional and personal judgments when assessing quality.

This anecdote demonstrates a major point about the concept of quality. Quality, like beauty, lies in the eye of the beholder.

WHAT IS QUALITY?

No universally accepted definition of the term *quality* exists; this is because quality actually possesses several distinct dimensions. When people disagree about what quality is, they are often simply demonstrating preferences for differing quality dimensions. The Federal Quality Institute (FQI) identifies a primary dimension of quality (performance) and several secondary dimensions: reliability, durability, conformance, availability, and timeliness (FQI, 1991, p. 2). Still other quality dimensions are recognized as particularly important in the human services, including accessibility, timeliness, consistency, humaneness, and results or outcomes (Patti, 1987; Pruger & Miller, 1991a). Some of these quality dimensions refer to characteristics of products and services; others refer to the staff or employees who provide the products and services; and still others refer to the facilities and equipment used in product production and service provision. A compilation of various quality dimensions, together with their definitions, is provided in Table 4.1.

Further complicating the discussion of quality is the problem that some quality dimensions can be antithetical in nature, meaning that an attempt to maximize one can lead to minimization of the other. For example, humaneness and consistency are frequently incompatible quality dimensions. Many bureaucracies—including, unfortunately, some in the human services—have a checkered history of dehumanizing both staff and clients through the blind pursuit of consistency. Nor are outcomes and accessibility necessarily complementary quality dimensions. The maximization of client outcomes is sometimes associated with a decrease in client accessibility. This phenomenon is generally referred to as client "creaming" (Hill, Blaser, & Balmer, 1986, p. 590; Williams & Webb, 1991, p. 108).

The research of Zeithaml et al. (1990) provides some guidance in dealing with the many dimensions of quality. Specifically, these researchers have attempted to reduce the many dimensions of quality down to a manageable number. Zeithaml et al. conducted extensive focus group interviews with nearly 2,000 customers representing a broad cross-section of service organizations. They were interested in determining the various dimensions of quality from the customer's perspective. The data derived from the focus group interviews were analyzed, using various statistical techniques. The researchers report

TABLE 4.1 Some Dimensions of Quality

Dimension	Definition
Accessibility	The product or service is easy to access or acquire.
Assurance	The staff are friendly, polite, considerate, and knowledgeable.
Communication	Customers are kept informed, in language they can understand, about the product or service and any changes thereto.
Competence	Staff possess the requisite knowledge and skills to provide the product or service.
Conformity	The product or service meets standards.
Courtesy	Staff politeness, respect, and consideration toward customers.
Deficiency	Any quality characteristic not otherwise identified that adversely affects customer satisfaction.
Durability	The performance, result, or outcome does not dissipate quickly.
Empathy	Staff demonstrate an understanding of and provide individualized attention to customers.
Humaneness	The product or service is provided in a manner that protects the dignity and self-worth of the customer.
Performance	The product or service does what it is supposed to do.
Reliability	The ability to provide the product or service in a dependable and consistent manner with minimal variation over time or between customers.
Responsiveness	The timeliness of employees in providing products and services.
Security	The product or service is provided in a safe setting and is free from risk or danger.
Tangibles	The physical appearance of facilities, equipment, personnel, and published materials.

SOURCES: Adapted from Zeithaml et al. (1990); FQI (1991); and Juran (1988).

TABLE 4.2 Five Major Quality Factors

1. Reliability
2. Responsiveness
3. Assurance
4. Empathy
5. Tangibles

SOURCE: Zeithaml et al. (1990, p. 27).

that they were able to reduce the various dimensions of quality down to five major factors. These five factors are identified in Table 4.2.

The results of Zeithaml et al.'s research also imply the existence of a quality dimension hierarchy. Their data suggest that the most important quality dimension to customers is reliability. Reliability means that customers form their quality expectations on the basis of the characteristics of past products and services, and that they expect to receive the same quality in future products and services. When too much variation creeps into product production or service provision, consumers perceive that quality problems exist.

The issue of the standardized meal menus used at most senior centers serves to illustrate the importance of reliability as a quality dimension. I once had the occasion to visit a senior center in rural Arizona that had just replaced its old meal menu with a new one. The old menu had been in place for about 2 years, and the senior center administrators thought it was time for a change. The administrators hadn't bothered, however, to ask the center's customers what they thought about making changes in the meal menu.

The customers had grown accustomed to the old menu and its scheduled bill of fare, including Mexican food every Friday. Under the new menu, new dishes were replacing old favorites, and Mexican food was scheduled to be served only one Friday a month. Shortly after the new menu was introduced, the number of customer complaints about the quality of the meals went up dramatically. Had the quality of the meals really declined? From a nutritional perspective and from the perspective of the senior center administration, the answer was "no." But from the customer's perspective, the answer was a definite "yes." The reliability of the meal experience had been broken by the new menu. The senior center customers equated this decline in reliability with an overall decline in the quality of the meals.

The finding that reliability is the most important quality dimension to customers also supports one of the major philosophical tenets of TQM: that variation lies at the heart of quality problems.

The next most important quality dimension to customers, according to Zeithaml et al. (1990), is responsiveness. Responsiveness refers to the timeliness of product or service provision. The importance of timeliness to consumers was brought home to me during an experience I had working in the out-patient section of a public hospital. Hospital management was concerned because customers consistently rated the quality of medical services as "low." After some research, we discovered that what was really bothering customers was the length of time they spent waiting to see a doctor. Customers were bothered by the timeliness of service delivery, which, in turn, was impacting their overall perceptions of the quality of medical care. As one might expect, when efforts were made to reduce waiting time, customers' perceptions of the quality of medical care began to improve.

The remaining three quality dimensions, according to Zeithaml et al. (1990), in declining order of importance, are assurance, empathy, and tangibles. Tangibles refers to the aesthetics, or appearance, of the buildings and equipment used in the production of products and the provision of services. Since many human service organizations do not operate out of the most attractive facilities or have access to the most up-to-date equipment, the fact that tangibles is the least important quality dimension to customers may be fortunate.

On a 100-point scale, the customers studied by Zeithaml et al. (1990, p. 29) assigned the following scores, or weights, to each of the five quality dimensions: reliability (32), responsiveness (22), assurance (19), empathy (16), and tangibles (11). Not only is reliability the most important quality dimension to customers, but it is also an order of magnitude greater than even the second most important dimension.

The quality dimensions and the quality hierarchy presented by Zeithaml et al. can be used by human service organizations to begin exploring the issue of quality in their own products and services. However, this research should probably not be accepted as definitive, because the focus groups did not include human service customers. Despite this deficiency, the five major quality factors do provide human service organizations with useful insights into, and a starting place for thinking about, quality.

Even if one accepts the research findings of Zeithaml et al., the question still remains: "What dimension or dimensions of quality are most important for human service organizations?" TQM theory provides a simple—yet complex—answer to this question. Ask your customers. In TQM, quality is determined, or defined, by customers.

CUSTOMER-DEFINED QUALITY

One of the areas of general agreement among the big four quality experts is that customers determine the relative importance of various quality dimensions (see Table 4.3). For example, Feigenbaum (1983, p. 7) states that quality means products and services that "meet the expectations of customers." Crosby (1985, p. 60) defines quality as "conformance to requirements." Since customers determine what the requirements are, according to Crosby, this is just another way of saying that customers define quality. Juran (1989, p. 360) states that quality is "fitness for use." As the customer determines whether a product or service is fit for use, this again is simply another way of saying that customers define quality.

Deming does not really define quality, but a definition can be inferred from his writings: the reduction of variation. Since variation is the cause of quality problems, the less variation—the higher the quality. Deming is unique in his view that quality is not defined solely by the customer. He maintains this posture because he believes that customers do not know all the various ways a product or service can be improved. Despite Deming's caveat, TQM takes the position that quality is primarily, if not exclusively, defined by customers.

The idea of customer-defined quality is considered a radical concept for many business and government organizations, but this should not be the case for human service organizations. Customer-defined quality actually represents a way of achieving the elusive human service and social work goal of putting the needs of clients first. However, the actual achievement of customer-defined quality in human service organizations can prove challenging because of the way human services have traditionally been conceptualized and funded.

Customer-defined quality poses at least four major challenges for human service organizations. First is the challenge of determining an organization's customers. Second is the challenge of reconciling different views on quality held by different classes of customers. Third is the long held tradition in the human services of quality being defined by professionals. Fourth is the challenge of collecting and using customer satisfaction data.

THE CHALLENGE OF DETERMINING
AN ORGANIZATION'S CUSTOMERS

When I ask administrators of human service organizations to identify who their customers are, the answer I usually get is "our clients."

TABLE 4.3 Definitions of Quality

Author	Definition
Crosby	Conformance to requirements
Juran	Fitness for use
Feigenbaum	Meeting customer expectations
Deming	Reduction in variation[a]

a. Not explicitly stated by Deming but inferred by the author from his works.

Clients, however, represent only one of several classes of customers, according to TQM theory. TQM theory suggests that all organizations have at least two classes of customers, while some—like human service organizations—may well have several.

In TQM, the concept of customer takes on a slightly different meaning—the beneficiaries of work (Koons, 1991, p. 17). TQM recognizes two major classes of customers, internal and external. An internal customer is any department, or unit, of an organization that receives products or services from another (Milakovich, 1990, p. 22). In applying the TQM notion of internal customers to a child welfare agency, for example, staff functions such as personnel and finance would be viewed as providing products and services to such programs (internal customers) as adoptions, residential treatment, day treatment, and the like.

The second class of customer (external) presents a more difficult conceptual challenge for human service organizations. The challenge here is that TQM assumes that all external customers are consumers, and vice versa. This assumption does not always hold for human service organizations (Baruch, 1984; Wagenheim & Reurink, 1991). Clients, for example, may consume the products or services of a human service organization, but not pay for them. Conversely, funding sources (e.g., government agencies, the United Way, and foundations) may pay for the products and services of a human service organization but not consume them. Thus, in reality, human service organizations have at least two classes of external customers. One class can be called *client* customers (Mills, 1990); the other can be referred to as *funding source* customers (Wagenheim & Reurink, 1991).

A practical solution to the challenge of multiple customers is to simply acknowledge that human service organizations are different, and to broaden the definition of external customer to be inclusive rather than exclusive (Milakovich, 1990). The Social Security Administration has done exactly this in deciding that it has two major categories of external customers: beneficiaries and the United States Congress (Carr & Littman, 1990, p. 29).

THE CHALLENGE OF RECONCILING
DIFFERENT CUSTOMER QUALITY VIEWS

The downside of broadening the definition of external customers is that different types of external customers may prefer different quality dimensions. Human service organizations receiving funding from the government, the United Way, or from foundations may discover that these funding sources have their own opinions about product and service quality. In the case of government funding, quality preferences may even be specified in law, statute, or regulation, or as a condition to a purchase of service contract. Thus, the concept of putting the needs of client customers first can be at odds with the golden rule of funding: "Whoever provides the gold makes the rules." The practical solution to this challenge is to simply recognize that human service organizations cannot operate without funding, and to give priority to funding source customer quality dimensions and standards. This position does not mean, however, that client-customer-defined quality dimensions and standards are ignored.

Client-customer-defined quality dimensions and standards can be used in areas where funding source customer requirements are nonexistent. Additionally, in areas where funding source customer quality standards do exist, they can be viewed as floors, and client-customer-defined standards raised above them. For example, senior centers receiving federal Older Americans Act funds for meal programs are required to ensure that each meal meets at least one third of the recommended daily allowance (RDA) of vitamins and minerals. All meals served must meet this standard. But other dimensions of meal quality are free to vary, including accessibility, tangibles, the courtesy of staff, and the responsiveness of the senior center toward providing special dietary and ethnic meals and celebrating special events such as holidays and birthdays.

Another example is in the area of child day-care services. All states have some sort of child day facility licensing and certification requirements. Standards exist, covering such areas as child-to-staff ratios, facility design, health and sanitation, food service, discipline, and so on. These standards must be met, but again they can be viewed as floors or minimums. Additionally, the type of curriculum offered, the types of toys and play equipment, the language abilities and ethnic backgrounds of the care workers (bilingual/bicultural, multilingual/multicultural) are all service quality dimensions that are free to vary, depending on client customer preferences.

THE CHALLENGE OF PROFESSIONALLY DEFINED QUALITY

Among the various classes of internal and external customers, one will not find a category for human service professionals. Professionals per se are not considered customers in TQM. Because they are not considered customers, professionals technically have no role in defining quality in TQM programs. This aspect of TQM runs counter to the long tradition in the human services of quality being defined by professionals. Again, some pragmatic adjustments may have to be made in order to apply TQM to human service organizations.

Quality, as defined by professional practice standards, licensure requirements, accreditation bodies, and so on, can be thought of as external customer-defined quality dimensions and standards. More problematic is the question of how to resolve quality issues when professional judgment is pitted against the expressed preferences of customers. Take, for example, the situation of the federal Job Training Partnership Act (JTPA) program. As expressed in both law and regulation, the JTPA program has a clear policy preference for job placements as the primary measure of service quality. Some human service professionals, on the other hand, argue that the JTPA program should place less emphasis on job placements and more emphasis on the quality dimension of program accessibility by serving more chronically unemployed and underemployed individuals. How can human service organizations reconcile conflicting quality views held by professionals and customers? Human service professionals are free to advocate and work for changes in the quality dimensions and standards specified in law and regulation, and to educate classes of external customers as to the pros and cons of certain quality dimensions and standards. The answer to this question, however, is quite clear: *Quality is defined by customers.*

THE CHALLENGE OF COLLECTING
AND USING CUSTOMER QUALITY DATA

The fourth major challenge to be dealt with in customer-defined quality is the collection and use of customer quality data. Table 4.4 illustrates a variety of approaches that can be used. The most common data collection technique is the customer satisfaction survey. The other

TABLE 4.4 Customer Quality Data Collection Techniques

1. Customer satisfaction survey	Customers are surveyed using mail, telephone, or face-to-face techniques.
2. Citizen or community surveys	Citizens are surveyed about a series of services usually provided by a unit of government.
3. Focus groups	Customers are brought together in small groups to discuss their likes and dislikes about a product or service.
4. Customer complaints	Detailed collection, tracking, and analysis of actual customer complaints.
5. Suggestion boxes	Customers can make anonymous suggestions and complaints.
6. Panels	A group of customers are routinely queried about their product and service likes and dislikes. (Differs from a focus group in that a panel is ongoing.)
7. Test marketing	A new product or service, or a change in a product or service, is tested first on a small group of actual customers in a small geographical area.

SOURCES: Adapted from Osborn and Gaebler (1992, pp. 177-179); Zeithaml et al. (1990, p. 55).

customer quality data techniques are used less frequently and are often employed as supplements to customer satisfaction surveys.

Focus groups represent a relatively inexpensive and quick method of gathering initial customer satisfaction data (Kruger, 1988; Morgan, 1988). Although data from focus group interviews are frequently referred to as *qualitative* data, the validity of focus group findings can be corroborated by subsequent *quantitative* data analysis of customer satisfaction surveys.

Chapter 5 explores in more detail the challenges involved in collecting and using customer satisfaction data.

Chapter 5

COLLECTING AND USING CUSTOMER QUALITY DATA

A human service organization can be driven by many different concerns. By being driven, I mean the nature of the force that provides the organization with its focus and direction. Forces that have been known to drive human service organizations include policy considerations, programming considerations, client considerations, financial considerations, management considerations, governing board considerations, and others. TQM is a customer quality driven management system. This means that a human service organization's focus and direction are provided by the quality preferences of its customers and ongoing attempts to satisfy those preferences.

A customer quality driven human service organization is one that (a) identifies the quality dimension preferences of its customers, (b) routinely collects quality data, and (c) uses the collected data to improve product and service quality. This may all sound rather complicated, but it really is not. By identifying the quality dimension preferences of customers, I simply mean determining what dimensions of quality (e.g., reliability, responsiveness, assurance, empathy, tangibles, or others) are important to an organization's customers, and how important. By customer quality data, I mean data on customers' perceptions of how well the organization is doing in satisfying their quality dimension preferences. An example may help make these points clearer.

Let us assume that the staff of a substance abuse program has surveyed its client customers and determined that the most important quality aspects of service delivery to them are how well staff treat them (empathy), not having to wait a long time for scheduled appointments (timeliness), and the success they are making in their treatment programs (performance). These three dimensions (empathy, timeliness, and performance) then constitute the quality dimension preferences of customers. Satisfying these preferences becomes the force that drives the organization.

To tell how well an organization is doing in satisfying the quality preferences of its customers, a system must be set up to routinely collect customer quality data. A customer satisfaction survey is frequently the approach of choice. In our substance abuse example, the customer quality data to be collected might consist of client perceptions over the period of the past 3 months as to how well staff has treated them (empathy), the number of times they have been kept waiting for more than 10 minutes for a scheduled appointment (timeliness), and how much progress they believe they have made in their treatment programs (performance).

The administrators of the substance abuse program would then analyze these data to ascertain how well the organization is doing in satisfying the quality dimension preferences of its customers. They would also seek to determine, at, say, 3-month intervals, if the organization appears to be doing a better job, a worse job, or staying about the same.

As Figure 5.1 illustrates, a customer quality driven organization can also be thought of as one that simply uses quality data as the feedback loop in a TQM system.

Regardless of the type of customer, internal or external, the tasks involved in collecting and using customer quality data are essentially the same. These tasks include (a) identifying the organization's customers, (b) determining customer quality preferences, (c) developing quality measures, (d) collecting quality data, and (e) monitoring quality data. In the following sections, each of these five tasks is described in more detail. The collection and use of internal customer quality data are dealt with first, followed by a discussion of collecting and using external client customer quality data. The discussion focuses initially on internal customer quality data, because when any new system is introduced into an organization, some problems and mistakes are inevitable. Consequently, a good place for human service organizations to begin experimenting with the collection and use of customer quality data is with internal customers. By beginning with internal customers, the inevitable problems and mistakes can be kept discreetly inside the organization. The lessons learned from working with internal customer quality data can then be applied to collecting and using external customer quality data.

Figure 5.1. Customer Quality Data as Feedback

COLLECTING AND USING
INTERNAL CUSTOMER QUALITY DATA

IDENTIFYING THE ORGANIZATION'S INTERNAL CUSTOMERS

The first task is to identify the organization's internal customers. Two concepts, *supplier/user* and *upstream/downstream*, are helpful in accomplishing this task. Internal customers in most human service organizations tend to be *downstream* users. In the language of TQM, a department, unit, or function of an organization is a *supplier* if its output becomes the input for another department, unit, or function—called a *user*. This relationship is illustrated in Figure 5.2.

Suppliers are upstream in a system or process flow; users are downstream. For example, the intake and eligibility determination functions for most human service organizations usually occur before the client customer is assigned either a case manager or provided service. Consequently, intake and eligibility determination are considered to be upstream from case management and direct service provision. Case management, on the other hand, is considered to be downstream from intake and eligibility determination, but is still upstream from direct service provision. When client customers complete the intake and eligibility determination processes, they represent an output for these units or functions. Client customers then proceed to the next stage of service delivery (e.g., case management), where they become the input for that unit or function.

The quality of the intake and eligibility determination processes in terms of such dimensions as reliability, responsiveness, and so on can directly affect the quality of the downstream (case management) unit's input. From this notion of one department, unit, or function's output becoming the input for another, TQM derives the notion of internal customers (Ishikawa, 1985).

A valuable tool in assisting human service organizations to identify their internal customers is the *supplier/user matrix* (Jessome, 1988, p. 249). The supplier/user matrix is designed to identify (a) all organiza-

Figure 5.2. The Systems Framework Applied to Internal Suppliers and Users

tional units (suppliers) that provide goods or services to other units, and (b) all organizational units (users or internal customers) that receive goods and services from other units. An example of a supplier/user matrix for a child welfare agency is shown in Figure 5.3. All departmental units of the organization are listed on both the horizontal (supplier) and vertical (user) axes. Departmental unit managers identify, by placing an O on the supplier/user matrix, all units they supply, and identify with an X all units that service them. As Figure 5.3 suggests, the staff functions of most human service organizations tend to be both suppliers and users; line functions tend to be primarily users. The supplier/user matrix not only serves to identify organizational suppliers and users, but also helps sensitize unit managers to their supplier/user and upstream/downstream relationships.

DETERMINING INTERNAL CUSTOMER QUALITY PREFERENCES

Once a human service organization has identified its internal customers, the next task is to determine their quality preferences. An effective tool in making this determination is the focus group (Albrecht, 1992). For our purposes, a focus group can be defined as a group interview, conducted with a cross-section of an organization's customers, for purposes of determining customer views on the quality of an organization's products and services. The optimum number of focus group participants is thought to be between 6 and 10 (Albrecht, 1992, p. 122; Morgan, 1988, p. 43).

Because different supplier units provide different products and services, separate focus group interviews would be convened for each identified supplier unit. In an informal setting, a facilitator engages the focus group participants in a general discussion about the products and services the supplier unit provides and what they consider to be quality in those products and services.

It is sometimes useful to rely on a prop to get the group focused. For example, I have found it helpful to use the five concepts of reliability, responsiveness, assurance, empathy, and tangibles as key trigger words to get focus group members thinking about quality and what quality means to them.

	Finance	Personnel	Clerical	Case Management	Day Treatment	Foster Care	Residential Treatment
Finance		X O	X O		X	X	X
Personnel	O		O		X	X	X
Clerical	O	O			X	X	X
Case Management	O	O	O		X	X	X
Day Treatment	O	O	O	O			
Foster Care	O	O	O	O			
Residential Treatment	O	O	O	O			

Figure 5.3. A Supplier/User Matrix for a Child Welfare Organization

If you have not participated in a focus group, let me attempt to briefly describe what one might look like. Let us assume that a focus group has been convened by a child welfare agency to define quality for the products and services provided by its finance unit. Seated around a circular table are six staff persons drawn from various user departments including personnel, clerical, case management, day treatment, foster care, and residential treatment. The facilitator begins by stating the objective of the focus group, that is, to determine what constitutes quality in the products and services of the finance unit. The facilitator might explain that the dimensions of reliability and responsiveness have been found to be important aspects of quality in other service areas. The facilitator might then ask each focus group member to explain what reliability and responsiveness mean to them in terms of the products and services provided by the finance unit. This process is continued until all five dimensions of quality have been discussed, as well as any other dimensions suggested by the focus group members. The facilitator ensures that all participants have an opportunity to express their opinions and that all opinions are considered. The focus group interview is continued until consensus is achieved among the participants as to what constitutes quality in the products and services of the finance unit.

Let us assume that the focus group members believe the most important quality dimensions of the work done by the finance unit are the correctness (reliability) and timeliness (responsiveness) of financial reports, contractor payments, and payroll processing.

DEVELOPING QUALITY MEASURES

Once internal customers have defined what quality means to them, the next task is to develop a method of measuring quality. There are two major approaches: (a) Quality indicators can be developed or (b) internal customer satisfaction can be assessed.

The Quality Indicator Approach. This approach involves two steps. First, one or more output measures are identified for each product and service that an internal supplier provides. Second, the output measures are then transformed into quality indicators by the addition of one or more quality dimension tests.

An output measure is a measure of work. For example, output or workload measures for the quality dimensions identified above for a human service organization's finance unit might be

1. the number of financial reports generated each month,
2. the number of contractor payments made each month, and
3. the number of payroll checks issued each month.

Table 5.1 demonstrates how these output measures can be transformed into quality indicators by adding reliability (accuracy) and responsiveness (timeliness) quality tests. By identifying the proportion of outputs that satisfy a quality test, a series of readily understandable quality indicators can be developed for any product produced or service provided by an internal supplier.

The Customer Satisfaction Approach. This approach involves developing a survey questionnaire and periodically surveying internal customers on their perceptions of the quality of internal suppliers' products and

TABLE 5.1 Quality Indicators for a Human Service Organization's Finance
                Department

1. Financial reports

    a. the percentage of financial reports issued error free each month.

    b. the percentage of financial reports issued on time each month.

2. Contractor payments

    a. the percentage of contractor payments issued error free each month.

    b. the percentage of contractor payments issued on time each month.

3. Payroll processing

    a. the percentage of payroll checks issued error free each month.

    b. the percentage of payroll checks issued on time each month.

services. Continuing with the example of a human service organization's finance unit, Table 5.2 is an example of an internal customer
satisfaction survey questionnaire. The survey questionnaire attempts
to tap internal customer perceptions about the accuracy (reliability) and
timeliness (responsiveness) of the finance unit's products and services.

The survey questionnaire includes an overall satisfaction question
and six more specific questions dealing with the accuracy and timeliness of financial reports, contractor payments, and payroll processing.
An actual internal customer survey questionnaire would include similar
questions for all the products and services provided by a supplier unit.
The purpose of the overall satisfaction question is so that statistical
techniques (e.g., correlation and regression analysis) can be used to
discover which products and services and which quality dimensions are
most important (are most highly associated with overall satisfaction) to
internal customers.

Once a set of questions and question wording is decided on, changes
should be discouraged. If questions or question wording is permitted to
vary from survey to survey, comparisons between surveys will not be
valid. One of the major advantages of using consumer satisfaction
surveys is the ability to monitor and track changes in consumer satisfaction levels over time.

COLLECTING QUALITY DATA

The next task involves creating a system to routinely collect and report
quality data. The collection and reporting of quality indicator data can be

TABLE 5.2 Finance Department User Satisfaction Survey

---

1. Overall, how satisfied are you with the products and services provided by the finance department?

Very dissatisfied				Very satisfied
1	2	3	4	5

2. Specifically, how satisfied are you with the overall accuracy of financial reports?

Very dissatisfied				Very satisfied
1	2	3	4	5

3. Specifically, how satisfied are you with the timeliness of financial reports?

Very dissatisfied				Very satisfied
1	2	3	4	5

4. Specifically, how satisfied are you with the accuracy of contractor payments?

Very dissatisfied				Very satisfied
1	2	3	4	5

5. Specifically, how satisfied are you with the timeliness of contractor payments?

Very dissatisfied				Very satisfied
1	2	3	4	5

6. Specifically, how satisfied are you with the accuracy of the payroll process?

Very dissatisfied				Very satisfied
1	2	3	4	5

7. Specifically, how satisfied are you with the timeliness of the payroll process?

Very dissatisfied				Very satisfied
1	2	3	4	5

---

done as frequently as monthly. Internal customer satisfaction surveys are more likely to be administered on a semiannual or quarterly basis.

The regular publication of quality data is important because it serves as a sort of report card to all user units (internal customers) and to top management on how well a service unit is performing. Beyond the report card function, supplier units operating in TQM environments also want to know how well they are doing managing their product and service quality.

TABLE 5.3 Finance Department Quality Indicator Report

	January	February	March	April
1. Financial reports				
a. Percentage issued error free	100	99	99	100
b. Percentage issued on time	100	100	100	100
2. Contractor payments				
a. Percentage issued error free	100	97	100	99
b. Percentage issued on time	92	87	83	80
3. Payroll processing				
a. Percentage payroll checks issued error free	100	100	98	100
b. Percentage payroll checks issued on time	100	100	100	100

MONITORING QUALITY DATA

The final task is to routinely monitor quality data to detect quality problems. Table 5.3 and Table 5.4 demonstrate how the monitoring of quality data provides feedback and insight into potential product and service quality problems.

Table 5.3 presents 4 months of hypothetical quality indicator data on the quality dimensions identified for a human service organization's finance unit. In general, the quality of the finance unit's products and services, as measured by the quality indicators, appears to be good. However, one notable exception to this statement is the timeliness of contractor payments. For each of the four reporting periods, the proportion of contractor payments made on time has decreased. The problem with the timeliness of contractor payments virtually leaps off the page and cries out for attention. The data do not identify what the quality problem is, but they do indicate where to look.

Table 5.4 presents some hypothetical data on the results of four consecutive internal customer satisfaction surveys of the same finance unit, using the questionnaire in Table 5.2. Overall satisfaction with the finance unit's products and services is rated relatively high by internal consumers, except for the timeliness of contractor payments. The satisfaction level of internal customers on this quality dimension has decreased steadily over the four survey periods. Also, overall satisfaction with the finance unit has decreased over the same period. This finding suggests that quality problems with the timeliness of contractor

TABLE 5.4 Finance Department Internal Consumer Satisfaction Survey Results

	Survey			
	1	2	3	4
1. Overall satisfaction	5.0	4.9	4.7	4.5
2. Satisfaction with accuracy of financial reports	5.0	5.0	5.0	5.0
3. Satisfaction with timeliness of financial reports	5.0	4.7	5.0	4.8
4. Satisfaction with accuracy of contractor payments	4.7	4.5	4.5	4.7
5. Satisfaction with timeliness of contractor payments	4.7	4.5	4.2	4.0
6. Satisfaction with accuracy of payroll preparation	4.5	4.5	4.7	4.5
7. Satisfaction with timeliness of payroll	4.7	4.5	4.5	4.5

NOTE: Range is 1 (*very dissatisfied*) to 5 (*very satisfied*).

payments may be affecting internal customer perceptions about the overall quality of the finance unit's products and services.

COLLECTING AND USING
CLIENT CUSTOMER QUALITY DATA

Having demonstrated how a human service organization can go about the tasks involved in collecting and using internal customer quality data, we can now discuss the collection and use of external client customer quality data. The tasks involved are the same: (a) identifying the organization's external client customers, (b) determining client customer quality preferences, (c) collecting customer quality data, and (d) monitoring customer quality data.

IDENTIFYING THE ORGANIZATION'S CLIENT CUSTOMERS

Considerable discussion was devoted in Chapter 2 to methods that human service organizations can use in identifying their client customers and will not be repeated here.

DETERMINING CLIENT CUSTOMER QUALITY PREFERENCES

The preferred method for collecting client customer quality data is the customer satisfaction survey. This section consequently focuses on the development and use of customer satisfaction surveys and the monitoring of the resulting quality data. As part of this discussion, a case example involving a specialized transportation service program is used to demonstrate how certain tasks might be accomplished.

In developing a customer satisfaction survey, the work of Zeithaml et al. (1990) and their five quality dimensions (reliability, responsiveness, assurance, empathy, and tangibles) can again be used as a starting point. A client customer satisfaction survey might consider tapping some, or perhaps all, of these five quality dimensions. Additionally, other important quality dimensions may exist, which are considered important by an organization's client customers in general or which may be uniquely important to a particular product or service.

All quality dimensions identified must be operationalized, that is, defined in quality dimension terms from the customer's perspective. For example, what does reliability mean to client customers of a specialized transportation service program or a child foster-care program? What does responsiveness mean to elderly client customers of an adult day-care center or a home-delivered meals program? What does assurance mean to client customers (parents) of a child day-care program? Focus group interviews are again an efficient method of sorting out and operationalizing (defining) quality dimensions. The results of focus group interviews can be used as the basis for developing a consumer satisfaction survey.

Let us assume that the administrators of a specialized transportation service (STS) program have conducted a series of focus group interviews with their riders. The STS administrators discover that some of Zeithaml et al.'s five quality dimensions are important to riders, but they need to be operationalized, or defined in quality dimension terms (e.g., reliability, responsiveness, assurance, empathy, tangibles, and others) with respect to service characteristics relevant to specialized transportation. Specifically, the STS administrators find the following quality dimensions to be most important to STS riders: on-time pickup (a measure of reliability), reservations availability (a measure of responsiveness), the friendliness and courtesy of STS drivers (a measure of assurance), and the driving skills of STS operators (a measure unique to transportation programs).

COLLECTING CUSTOMER QUALITY DATA

Having identified the quality dimension preferences of client customers, the next task is to develop a system for the routine collection of client customer quality data. The accomplishment of this task includes developing and field-testing a survey questionnaire and setting up a system to periodically survey client customers. The case example of the specialized transportation service (STS) program can again be used to demonstrate how a human service organization might go about these activities.

Using the information and insights gained from the focus group interviews, let us assume that STS administrators draft a customer satisfaction survey questionnaire and field-test it. Some changes in questionnaire wording are made as a result of the field test. The questionnaire contains several quality questions and several respondent demographic questions. The service quality questions are shown in Table 5.5. The questionnaire contains one question dealing with client customers' overall perceptions of quality with the STS program, and four more specific questions dealing with specific quality dimensions. As was the case with the internal customer satisfaction survey questionnaire discussed earlier, the inclusion of an overall satisfaction question is done so that subsequent statistical analysis can tell which quality dimensions have the most impact on perceptions of overall quality.

While no hard-and-fast rules exist governing how frequently a client customer satisfaction survey should be conducted, at a minimum one should probably be conducted at least annually, and more frequently (semiannually or quarterly) if possible. Each survey must involve a sufficiently large sample of client customers to insure reasonable confidence in the resulting data. The same questions also need to be used from survey to survey so that comparisons can be made over time. The resulting data from client customer satisfaction surveys should be routinely reported so that citizens, policymakers, external funding source customers, administrators, and client customers know how well the organization is doing in managing the quality of its products and services.

MONITORING CUSTOMER QUALITY DATA

Having conducted a client customer satisfaction survey, the next step is to monitor the results. Continuing with the case example of the Specialized Transportation Service (STS) program, Table 5.6 presents some actual data on STS client customer (rider) responses to the five quality questions identified in Table 5.5. The data are drawn from a series of customer (rider) satisfaction surveys conducted by the Maricopa County (Phoenix, Arizona) Department of Social Services.

Some 95% of client customers (riders) report that overall they are "very satisfied" with the STS program. This statistic appears to support the conclusion that the STS program is operating well. But is this an accurate interpretation? What exactly does a 95% satisfaction rate

TABLE 5.5 Specialized Transportation Services Consumer Satisfaction Questionnaire

---

1. Overall, how satisfied are you with
   special transportation services?
      1. Very satisfied
      2. Somewhat satisfied
      3. Dissatisfied
      4. Very dissatisfied
2. Do you usually get reservations for the days you need?
      1. Almost always
      2. Usually
      3. Seldom
      4. Almost never
3. Are you usually picked up on time?
      1. Almost always
      2. Usually
      3. Seldom
      4. Almost never
4. In general, how do you rate the driving skills of the STS drivers?
      1. Excellent
      2. Good
      3. Fair
      4. Poor
5. In general, how do you rate the attitude
   (friendliness and courtesy) of STS drivers?
      1. Excellent
      2. Good
      3. Fair
      4. Poor

---

mean? Is this an above-average rating for a specialized transportation service program? What is missing in order to accurately interpret this statistic is some sort of benchmark.

Benchmarking. Benchmarking can be defined as the comparison of products, services, work processes, and other measures against best practices in the field (Spendolini, 1992, p. 9). The purpose of benchmarking is to provide a basis for comparison and to learn. There are two general approaches to benchmarking, competitive and internal (Spendolini, 1992).

TABLE 5.6 STS Client Customer Satisfaction Survey Data

	Number	*Percentage*
1. Overall, how satisfied are you with special transportation services?		
1. Very satisfied	321	95.0
2. Somewhat satisfied	14	4.1
3. Dissatisfied	1	.3
4. Very dissatisfied	2	.6
	338	100
. 2. Do you usually get reservations for the days you need?		
1. Almost always	281	85.2
2. Usually	40	12.1
3. Seldom	6	1.8
4. Almost never	3	.9
	330	100
3. Are you usually picked up on time?		
1. Almost always	274	82.5
2. Usually	48	14.5
3. Seldom	5	1.5
4. Almost never	5	1.5
	332	100
4. How do you rate the driving skills of STS drivers?		
1. Excellent	258	76.6
2. Good	71	21.1
3. Fair	6	1.8
4. Poor	2	.6
	337	100
5. How do you rate the attitude (friendliness and courtesy) of STS drivers?		
1. Excellent	275	81.1
2. Good	58	17.1
3. Fair	5	1.5
4. Poor	1	.3
	339	100

SOURCE: Maricopa County Department of Social Services (1985).

Competitive Benchmarking. This is where an organization's products and services are compared with those of other organizations—particularly those that represent the best practices in the field. Thus a specialized transportation program could benchmark its client customer satisfaction rates against the rates of other programs, especially those considered to be leaders in the field. In order to use competitive benchmarking, two obstacles must be overcome—identifying best practice organizations and convincing them to share information.

Frequently, a human service organization may be the only one of its kind in a geographical area, and thus may have no comparable organization to benchmark against. Some attempts have been made to develop norms for customer satisfaction ratings (e.g., Miller & Miller, 1991), but these norms are national averages that may not be totally applicable either to any specific geographical area or to a particular category of client customer. These obstacles may make internal benchmarking a more attractive alternative for many human service organizations.

Internal Benchmarking. Internal benchmarking is where an organization benchmarks against itself. For example, a program or service could benchmark itself against another program or service provided by the same organization. Likewise, if an organization is departmentalized on the basis of region, a program or service in one region can benchmark itself against a program or service in another region. In the case example of the STS program, client consumer (rider) satisfaction rates in one geographical region can be benchmarked against those of another region that is generally considered to be an example of best practices within the program.

Another approach to internal benchmarking is to compare client consumer satisfaction rates over time. After a client customer satisfaction survey has been conducted several times, response rates can be compared between surveys to detect increases or decreases in the quality perceptions of client customers over time (Mossard, 1991, p. 233).

Overreporting. Overreporting is an issue to consider when attempting to benchmark and interpret client customer quality data. Many client customers depend on the programs and services they receive to help them meet basic needs and maintain an independent life-style. When human service organizations ask client customers if they are satisfied with the products and services they receive, there may be a tendency to respond favorably for fear that negative responses might place the program or service at risk.

How can human service administrators spot potential overreporting on client customer satisfaction surveys? One method is to compare overall satisfaction rates with data gathered on other quality dimension questions. Referring again to Table 5.6, only 85% of client customers (riders) surveyed indicate they are able to get reservations for the days they need. This finding may indicate some potential quality problem with the

TABLE 5.7 STS Client Consumer (Rider) Satisfaction Surveys

Service Quality Dimension	Modal Response Category	Proportion Responding (percentages)				
		Survey 1	Survey 2	Survey 3	Survey 4	Survey 5
Overall satisfaction	Very satisfied	95.0	93.4	80.1	74.2	95.3
Reservations availability	Almost always	85.2	89.1	83.3	82.0	95.9
On-time pickup	Almost always	82.5	80.2	74.3	77.3	86.2
Drivers' skills	Excellent	76.6	74.8	76.2	72.8	82.8
Drivers' attitudes	Excellent	81.1	81.3	80.3	81.6	82.6

SOURCE: Maricopa County Department of Social Services (1985).

reservation system. Likewise, only 82% of client customers say they are usually picked up on time, indicating a potential quality problem with the scheduling system. And only 76% and 81% of client customers, respectively, rate the skills and attitudes of STS drivers as excellent. This finding may be indicative of potential quality problems in the recruitment, selection, and training of drivers. Thus, while client customers (riders) maintain that overall they are "very satisfied" with the STS program, when more detailed questions are asked about specific quality dimensions, less satisfaction is demonstrated. The data do not indicate what the potential quality problems are, but they do indicate where to look.

A final comment about monitoring client customer satisfaction quality data concerns what happens to human service organizations who discover that the quality of their products and services is high, and then decide to rest on their laurels. Resting on one's laurels is not a part of TQM. American management theory suggests that "if it ain't broke, don't fix it." The equivalent TQM axiom is that "unattended systems tend to run down." The only way to keep a system operating at peak performance is to be constantly seeking ways to improve it.

The problems that human service organizations can find themselves in by resting on their laurels, rather than constantly attempting to improve the quality of their products and services, is amply demonstrated by what actually happened to the Specialized Transportation Service (STS) program operated by the Maricopa County Department of Social Services. Table 5.7 shows the results of five consecutive client customer (rider) satisfaction surveys conducted at approximately 6-month intervals.

Data from the first two satisfaction surveys (S1 and S2) suggested that client customers were "very satisfied" overall with the program. The administrators became complacent and did not seek to improve quality further, or even to ensure that current quality levels were maintained. The third survey (S3) showed a dramatic decline in overall client customer (rider) satisfaction. After the fourth survey (S4), the program administrators realized they had a crisis on their hands and finally began to work on improving quality again. The fruits of their labors were amply rewarded in the next survey (S5), where the overall satisfaction rate rebounded to a 95% "very satisfied" level.

This case example provides some hard evidence in support of the need for continuous quality improvement. Variation is the cause of most quality problems. Consequently, understanding and reducing variation in product production and service delivery systems and major processes is key to improving quality. The following chapter deals with the subject of understanding and reducing variation.

Chapter 6

UNDERSTANDING AND CONTROLLING VARIATION

One of the key elements of TQM as a philosophy of management is its focus on understanding and controlling variation. Variation can be defined as any deviation from standard. TQM is concerned with the study, comprehension, prediction, and control of variation in systems and processes.

Variation is the natural enemy of quality. Quality suffers when too much variation is present in the processes used to produce products and provide services. The point has been made several times that reliability may well be the single most important quality dimension to customers. Reliability means that the quality of products and services is consistently the same over time. As Figure 6.1 illustrates, variation in processes sets up a causal chain that affects reliability, which in turn affects quality.

For human service organizations, reliability means that each time a customer (internal or external) has contact with the organization: (a) the experience should be essentially the same, (b) the product received should be essentially the same, and (c) the service received should be essentially the same. When these conditions are satisfied, the concept of reliability suggests that customers will perceive the quality of products and services to be high. When these conditions are not met, customers may well perceive that quality has deteriorated. The key to ensuring reliability and maintaining quality in any organization lies in controlling the variation in processes.

TQM's concern with understanding and controlling variation does not mean that human service professionals are prohibited from individualizing and personalizing when dealing with customers. What it does

53

VARIATION ——————→ RELIABILITY ——————→ QUALITY

Figure 6.1. The Effect of Variation on Quality

mean is that one always has to smile, to greet people warmly, to start on time, to keep promises, and so on. Customers must believe that you will be there for them and treat them honestly, openly, fairly, and consistently. One must also refrain from experimenting with alternative methods of product production or service provision when the organization has a standardized approach. Standardization can be thought of as a floor, the minimum, that must be satisfied in all product production and service provision. Above the floor, individualization and personalization are allowable and may even be encouraged. In fact, variation can be an important aspect of quality. The creative use of variation is why we take kids on field trips out of school, why we shut down normal programming in a community center and have a party, why we have an end-of-the-year picnic with kids in foster placements, and so on.

THE NATURE OF VARIATION

According to the majority of American TQM experts, variation is naturally present in all processes. Variation, they suggest, can be controlled and reduced but never totally eliminated. A dissenting voice is Crosby (1980), who believes that variation in processes can be totally eliminated, as suggested by his slogan "zero-defects." Setting aside the debate over whether variation can be reduced to absolute zero, all the major American quality experts do agree that variation in processes must be understood and reduced.

For purposes of illustrating how variation can affect quality in a human service organization, consider the situation of two children in a day-care center. The two children can spend the same number of hours in the center on the same day, but variation can result in the quality of their day-care experiences being markedly different. Variation can be caused by differences in the education, training, attitudes, and concern of workers, or by facility and equipment problems, or by other factors.

In the language of TQM, variation is said to have two primary causes, common and special (Carr & Littman, 1990, pp. 73-74; Gitlow et al., 1989, p. 163; Provost & Norman, 1990, p. 42). As Table 6.1 suggests, *common causes* of variation are small random sources that are always

TABLE 6.1   Major Types of Variation

Common causes—Causes that *are* inherent in processes and affect all workers and all product production and service provision
Special causes—Causes that *are not* inherent in processes, but arise due to specific circumstances

SOURCE: Provost and Norman (1990, p. 42).

present in any process or system; *special causes* of variation are non-random and are caused by sources outside the system or process.

Examples of common causes of variation are when a machine or vehicle breaks down, or when the air-conditioning in your office goes out, or when you show up late for an appointment because it rained that day and you got stuck in traffic. These common, or random, occurrences affect the quality of our products and services, but they are forces that are usually beyond our ability to control. Examples of special causes of variation are when a new employee makes a series of mistakes because the job is still unfamiliar, or when an experienced employee makes several mistakes because of experimentation with an unauthorized approach to performing some task. Special causes of variation can be controlled. In these two examples, the new employee might be given some additional training and the experienced employee might be discouraged from unauthorized experimentation. Special causes of variation are said to be outside the system or process because they were caused by employees deviating from standards.

Common causes, or systems problems, are said to account for 85% of the variation in most processes. This is the famous 85/15 rule. Two major TQM axioms are derived from the 85/15 rule: (a) Individual employee appraisal is destructive, and (b) the overwhelming majority of quality problems are due to shortcomings of management, not employees.

TQM takes a dim view of the traditional American management practice of individual performance appraisal. TQM argues against the individual approach to evaluation, motivation, and rewards because it is predicated on the false notion that employees have control over the variation in their work environments. If 85% of variation in processes is due to common causes, and if common causes are due to systems problems, then only 15% of the variation in processes can be attributed to employees. In other words, TQM theory suggests that individual workers have little control over their jobs. They are simply working within systems created by management. If this argument is true, and TQM theory states that it is, individually focused evaluations place an organization's employees in the position of being held accountable for factors beyond their control.

The implication of the 85/15 rule for motivation and performance appraisal in organizations is that team and group approaches are preferred over individual approaches. While still a somewhat novel idea, team and group performance appraisal and reward systems can be designed and successfully implemented (Lawler, 1990; Motorola, 1992; Osborn & Gaebler, 1992; Peters & Austin, 1985; Zeithaml et al., 1990).

The second TQM axiom that flows from the 85/15 rule is that most variation occurs because the system is not being properly managed. According to TQM theory, an organization must be viewed as a totality—in other words, as a system. The primary job of management is to manage the system.

One of the tenets that distinguishes TQM from traditional American management is the notion that "unattended systems tend to run down." One implication of this tenet is that the status of major system processes must be constantly monitored and fine-tuned. Human service administrators working in TQM environments should be able at all times to answer two fundamental questions: Are the major processes involved in the production of my products and the provision of my services under control? And, is the quality of my products and services getting better, worse, or staying about the same?

How can human service administrators know when the major processes involved in product production and service provision are under control? The answer is, when all major processes are stabilized. Stable processes are considered to be under control; unstable processes are considered to be out of control. A stable process is one where the common causes of variation are within acceptable standards, and where special causes of variation are not operating.

DETERMINING IF A PROCESS IS UNDER CONTROL

The remainder of this chapter deals with applying TQM concepts and tools to determining if major system processes are under control. This determination involves three major activities. First, the product production or service delivery system is defined. Second, the major system processes are identified. Third, the status (stable/unstable) of all major system processes is determined. Two TQM tools are introduced for the first time as part of this analysis: the systems flow chart and the process control chart.

DEFINING THE SYSTEM

The first major activity involved in determining if all major system processes are under control is to define the system. Any product produced or service provided by a human service organization can be treated as a system. A system is defined by flow charting all its processes. Flow charts facilitate an understanding of systems by providing a visual display that identifies the various constituent processes and their interrelationships. Continuing with the ongoing case example of a specialized transportation service (STS) program, a simplified flow chart showing the system's processes is shown in Figure 6.2.

Standardized symbols are used to develop and facilitate understanding of system flow charts. Figure 6.3 illustrates the major flow chart symbols. While a detailed discussion of flow charting is beyond the scope of this chapter, some simple guidelines do exist (see Table 6.2).

DETERMINING THE MAJOR PROCESSES

Once a system is defined, the next activity involves identifying the system's major processes. In TQM, a system's major processes are (a) the ones with the greatest potential for variation and instability and (b) those most visible to customers. By focusing on a system's major processes, TQM attempts to avoid the problem of suboptimization, which occurs when resources are expended to improve noncritical processes while other more critical processes go unattended (Brinkerhoff & Dressler, 1990, p. 49).

As an aid in identifying a system's major processes, Sheer (1991) suggests asking the following questions: What processes generate the most customer complaints? What processes generate the most errors? What processes appear unpredictable? What processes contain bottlenecks where product or service flow slows down, creating queues and backlogs?

Another method of identifying a system's major processes is called *blueprinting* (Albrecht, 1992; George & Gibson, 1991). Blueprinting refers to the analysis of a system to identify those processes that are visible to customers. Customer visible processes are denoted in blue, or set above a blue line, on a system flow chart, hence the term *blueprinting*. Customer visible processes are considered to have more impact on customer quality perceptions than nonvisible processes. Albrecht (1992, p. 159) considers customer visible processes to be so important that he refers to them as "quality critical processes."

Still another way to identify a system's most important processes is to relate variation in customer satisfaction levels to variation in system

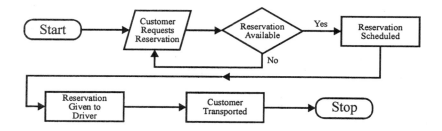

Figure 6.2. A Flow Chart of the STS Program

processes. Through statistical analyses using correlation, regression, and other routines, determinations can be made as to the most important processes in terms of their effect on overall customer satisfaction levels. This approach was discussed in Chapter 5.

An analysis of the flow chart in Figure 6.2 reveals that the transport process is the only customer visible process. The other processes all take place outside the view of customers. Thus, blueprinting suggests that the transport process has a high potential for influencing customer quality perceptions. Let us assume that STS administrators have evaluated client customer (rider) complaints and have conducted a statistical analysis of client customer satisfaction survey data. This additional research also indicates that client customers (riders) place considerable emphasis on the transport process in assessing the overall quality of the STS program.

DETERMINING IF A MAJOR PROCESS IS STABLE

The stability of a process is determined by use of the second TQM tool to be introduced—the process control chart. A process control chart is a statistical and visual method of studying a process to determine if common causes of variation are within normal tolerances and to ascertain if any special causes of variation are affecting the process. Process control charts are sometimes referred to as Shewart charts, after the man who first developed them (Juran, 1988, p. 348). Table 6.3 identifies the steps involved in collecting and analyzing data using process control charts. Each of these steps may be best explained by applying them to our continuing case example of a specialized transportation service (STS) program.

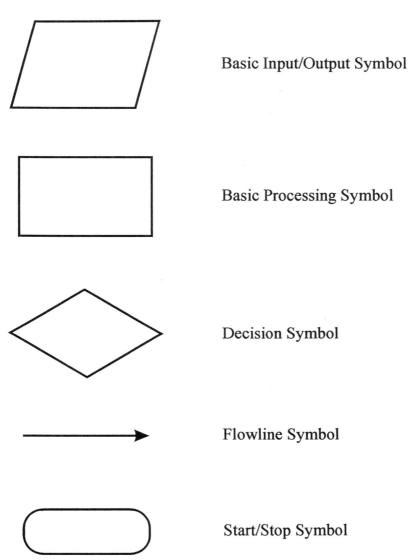

Figure 6.3. Standardized Flow Chart Symbols

Step 1: Identifying a process characteristic to study. Identifying a process characteristic to study usually means identifying what constitutes a defect,

TABLE 6.2   Ten Rules for Constructing Flow Charts

---

1. Identify all steps in the process.

2. Sequence all activities in their proper order.

3. Label all activities with simple descriptors (e.g., client interviewed, client determined eligible, client referred).

4. Draw the flow chart, working from top to bottom, and from left to right.

5. Use standard flow charting symbols.

6. Use simple symbols rather than more complex symbols.

7. Ensure that each path in the process flow leads to another activity symbol. If a path dead-ends, it should be noted with the "stop" symbol.

8. All symbols, except for decisions, should have only one output path.

9. Decision symbols are always binary in nature, with two output paths, a "yes" path and a "no" path.

10. Use connector symbols to connect multiple pages of a flowchart or to identify subsystems appearing on different pages.

SOURCES: Adapted from Gitlow et al. (1989, pp. 46-47) and Brassard (1988, p. 13).

or error, in a process. For example, a defect or error could be an incorrect eligibility determination, an inappropriate referral, an over-payment of general assistance, a senior center meal that fails to meet one third of the RDA, a home-delivered meal that arrives cold, or any other deviation from a prescribed standard established by a human service organization.

Let us assume that focus group interviews and the analysis of cus-tomer satisfaction survey data reveal that on-time pickup is the most important performance measure for the transport process. Being picked up late can be considered a "defect," or a deviation from standard. Late pickups then become the process characteristic to be studied.

Step 2: Determining the type of process control chart to be used. While there are a number of different process control charts that are used by business and government, the two that probably have the most rele-vance for human service organizations are the *c-chart* and the *np-chart*. When the process being studied has a small number of infrequently occurring defects, then the c-chart is used; in other instances, the np-chart can be used. The construction of an np-chart requires the drawing of a series of random samples of the process, and the compu-tation of the number of defects. The c-chart is constructed using the number of defects found in a "constant area of opportunity."

Because it is probably the easiest process control chart to use, let us apply the c-chart to the study of late pickups (a defect) in the transport

TABLE 6.3   Major Steps in Developing and Analyzing a Process Control Chart

Step 1—Identifying a process characteristic to study
Step 2—Determining the type of process control chart to be used
Step 3—Establishing baseline data on defect rates
Step 4—Computing the average defect rate
Step 5—Creating the process control chart
Step 6—Plotting the data on the process control chart
Step 7—Determining if the process is stable or unstable

function of our STS program. At the end of this discussion, we will return to the slightly more complex subject of the np-chart.

The c-chart is the easiest process control chart to use because it does not require drawing samples. Instead, it requires that the defect rate be computed over a "constant area of opportunity." For purposes of the human services, a constant area of opportunity can be thought of as a standardized time element. The number of defects occurring in a process during some predetermined and constant time frame are counted and compared over time. The time frame can be a minute, an hour, a day, a week, or any other standard time element.

The time frame, however, must not vary. For example, if an hour is chosen as the standard time element, each hour must always consist of exactly 60 minutes, so that the defect being studied has an equal opportunity of occurring in each hour. This same caution applies to the adoption of any standard time element, and particularly to the use of a week as the standard time element. A week containing 5 working days can not be compared to a week of 4 or 6 working days, because the defect has more chances to occur in a 5- or 6-day work week than in a 4-day work week. A major hurdle in using a week as a standard time frame is the problem of holidays. If a human service program operates on holidays, there may be no problem; but if the program closes down for holidays, then using a week as a standard frame may not be possible.

Step 3: Establishing baseline data on the defect rate. Continuing with our case example of the STS program, let us assume that the STS administrators decide to use a c-chart to study and control late pickups (a defect) in the STS transport process. The defect rate, the number of customers (riders) picked up late, can be expressed as a whole number, and the constant area of opportunity is established as one week. All that remains for the STS administrators to do in order to complete a c-chart is record the number of actual late pickups each week. Table 6.4

TABLE 6.4 Establishing Center Line and Upper and Lower Control Limits for a "C" Process Control Chart

Week	Number of Late Pickups
1	3
2	7
3	2
4	6
5	4
6	3
7	5
8	4
9	7
10	9
	50

Computation of center line $\dfrac{\text{Number of defects}}{\text{Number of weeks}} = \dfrac{50}{10} = 5$

Computation of UCL(c) = $c + 3\sqrt{c} = 5 + 6.7 = 11.7$
Computation of LCL(c) = $c - 3\sqrt{c} = 5 - 6.7 = 0$

presents some hypothetical data on the number of late pickups for a period of 10 consecutive weeks.

Step 4: Computing the average defect rate. The average defect rate is the mean, or numeric average, of late pickups for the study period (10 weeks). As Table 6.4 illustrates, the average defect rate is computed by taking the total number of riders picked up late (50) and dividing by the number of weeks involved (10). The average defect rate is 5.

Step 5: Creating the process control chart. In this case, our process control chart is going to be a visual display of the number of defects (riders picked up late) that occurred each week during the 10-week period being studied. As Figure 6.4 illustrates, the y, or horizontal, axis of a process control chart is usually denoted as time; the x, or vertical, axis is usually the characteristics being studied (Juran, 1989, p. 161). In this example, the x axis is a count of the number of riders picked up late, or the defect rate.

The average defect rate becomes the center line (c) for the process control chart. In this example, the center line is 5. Next, the upper control limit (UCL) and the lower control limit (LCL) are computed. These two limits are generally three standard errors from the center line.

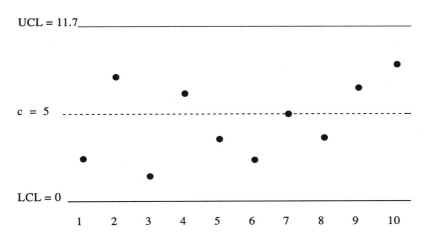

Figure 6.4. A Process Control C-Chart for Late Pickups

The lowest possible LCL for any process control chart is zero. An LCL can never be a negative number; the UCL is unbounded. The formulas shown in Table 6.4 can be used to determine the UCL and the LCL for any c-chart. From the formulas, we determine that the UCL for our c-chart is 11.7, and the lower control limit is 0, because the LCL cannot be a negative number. Because the UCL includes a fraction of a number (11.7), 11 defects would be considered within the boundary, while 12 defects would be considered outside the boundary. The UCL and LCL define the boundaries of a stable process, one that is under control.

Step 6: Plotting the data on the process control chart. This step involves plotting the characteristic being studied—in this case the number of riders picked up late (the defect rate) for each week. Figure 6.4 also shows the plot of these data.

Step 7: Determining if the process is stable or unstable. The UCL and LCL of a process control chart are based on the variation that occurs within samples. Between sample variation is excluded from the analysis. Because of this approach, if special causes of variation are present in a process, they are visually highlighted by the process control chart (Gitlow et al., 1989, p. 168). Special causes of variation are nonrandom occurrences. When special causes of variation are absent in a process, the data points plotted on a process control chart appear random. When special causes of variation are present in a process, the data points exceed the UCL, or the LCL, or they form patterns. Determining if a process is stable or unstable involves two tests for the presence of special causes of variation. The first test involves determining if all the data points fall within the UCL and the LCL. The second test involves analyzing the data points for the presences of patterns.

If any of the data points on a process control chart fall above the UCL or below the LCL, then special causes of variation are said to be present and the process is considered to be unstable. In the case of our c-chart shown in Figure 6.5, all data points fall within the UCL and the LCL. Thus, the STS transport process meets the first test for stability. What this means is that the number of late pickups (the defect rate) from week to week is what would be naturally expected on the basis of random variation.

The second test for the presence of special causes of variation involves looking for patterns in the data. Patterns are nonrandom occurrences and also reflect special causes of variation at work. The three most common patterns (trend, jump, and cycle) are illustrated in Figure 6.5.

When we examine the c-chart in Figure 6.4 for patterns, some evidence of a minor trend is apparent. Over the last 3 weeks the number of riders picked up late has increased. This pattern suggests the presence of some type of special cause of variation in the process. It might well be that a new driver is responsible for the pattern in late pickups as he learns the routes. The appearance of three increasing or decreasing data points on a process control chart is not sufficient, however, to declare a process unstable. The guideline is that eight consecutive data points must increase or decrease before a process should be declared unstable and out of control (Gitlow et al., 1989, p. 194). Nevertheless, an apparent trend of this nature does warrant close monitoring.

At the beginning of this chapter the suggestion was made that human service administrators working in a TQM environment should be able to answer two fundamental questions: Are the major system processes involved in the production of my products and the provision of my services under control? And, is the quality of my products and services getting better, worse, or staying about the same? In the case of our STS transport process, the answer to the first question is "yes." However, because the number of defects has been trending upwards over the last 3 weeks, the answer to the second question is "no."

Let us turn our attention now to a discussion of np-charts. Again, the np-chart can be used when the requirements of the c-chart cannot be satisfied. Construction of an np-chart is based on a series of sample data. Sample sizes must be constant; the number in one sample cannot vary from the number in another. Let us assume that, based on the

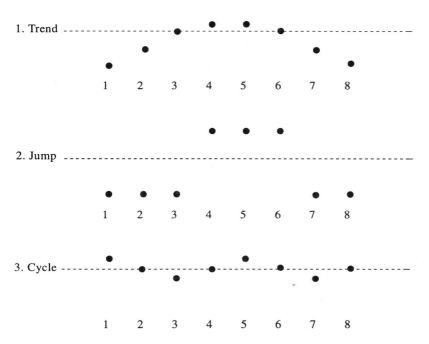

Figure 6.5. Patterns in Process Control Charts Due to Special Causes of Variation

number of customer (rider) complaints, STS administrators believe the number of late pickups, (the defect) in any given week is a significant number. For the next 10 weeks, a random, and constant size, sample of 100 customers (riders) is drawn each week from the drivers' logs, and a determination is made as to the number picked up late. Table 6.5 presents the resulting data.

As Table 6.5 illustrates, the average number of defects per sample is 13, which becomes the center line for our np-chart (see Figure 6.6). The UCL and the LCL for our np-chart are computed at three standard errors above and below the center line; the UCL is set at 23.1, the LCL at 2.9. Because the UCL and LCL are not whole numbers, the number of defects per sample would have to be 24 to be outside the UCL and 2 or less to be outside the LCL. The formulas shown in Table 6.5 can be used to compute the UCL and the LCL for any np-chart.

As the np-chart in Figure 6.6 shows, the UCL limits were breached on two separate occasions, during Week 5 and again during Week 8.

TABLE 6.5   Establishing Center Line and Upper and Lower Control Limits for an "NP" Process Control Chart

Week		Sample Size	Number of Late Pickups
1		100	9
2		100	12
3		100	11
4		100	8
5		100	25
6		100	16
7		100	10
8		100	26
9		100	8
10		100	5
	Totals	1,000	130

Computation of center line $np = \dfrac{\text{Number of defects}}{\text{Number of samples}}$

$$np = \frac{130}{10} = 13$$

$$UCL(np) = np + 3\sqrt{np(1-p)} = 13 + 3\sqrt{13(1-.13)} = 23.1$$

$$LCL(np) = np - 3\sqrt{np(1-p)} = 13 - 3\sqrt{13(1-.13)} = 2.9$$

NOTE: np = the average defect rate per sample (e.g., 13) and p = the average defect rate per sample divided by the common sample size (e.g., 13/100 = .13).

Because these two data points fall outside the UCL, the transport process in this example would be considered unstable. Some form of special variation was operating on these 2 days. The challenge for management is to find out what it was. Management might also be interested in exploring why it is that during Week 10 there were only five late pickups. A process control chart not only identifies where the problems are, but also highlights where exemplary activity took place.

No trends, cycles, or jumps are evident in the data, so it appears that special causes of variation are not affecting the process in this fashion.

This completes our discussion of process control charts. For more information on other types of process control charts and their uses, the reader is directed to Gitlow et al. (1989) and Rosander (1989), both of whom provide comprehensive treatments of the subject.

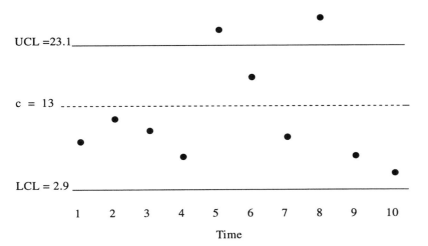

Figure 6.6. A Process Control NP-Chart for Late Pickups

AFTER MAJOR PROCESSES ARE STABILIZED

After all the major processes in a system are stabilized, a human service organization does not sit back and relax. Stabilization of a major process is only the first step in what TQM calls continuous quality improvement. Using the norms developed by process control charts as points of departure, or baselines, a human service organization next begins the ongoing and never ending quest of continually improving major system processes by continually reducing variation.

In the next chapter, the TQM approaches and tools used in the ongoing pursuit of reduced variation and the continuous pursuit of quality improvement are discussed.

Chapter 7

CONTINUOUS QUALITY IMPROVEMENT THROUGH TEAMWORK

Another basic tenet of TQM as a philosophy of management is the notion of continuous quality improvement through teamwork. These twin notions, continuous change and teamwork, again illustrate the difference between TQM and traditional American management.

Traditional American management theory tends to view change as being radical in nature and occurring in quantum leaps. Change comes about as the result of "breakthroughs" created by the application of new technologies (Carr & Littman, 1990) or by "champions" who engage the bureaucracy in individual combat to promote their ideas (Peters & Waterman, 1982). Change in TQM is constant and, consequently, tends to be incremental in nature. TQM makes no allowance for "cowboy" management, as the Japanese are fond of referring to some traditional American management practices (Imai, 1986).

The old fable of the race between the tortoise and the hare is an appropriate metaphor for understanding the differing views of change and quality improvement implicit in traditional American management theory and TQM. Change in TQM tends to be slow and plodding, but in the end—successful.

The team focus of TQM should be appealing to many human service professionals, because cooperation replaces competition as the interpersonal value to be maximized. Downplaying individual competition may also facilitate the integration of "differently abled" employees into the work forces of human service organizations (Power, 1991).

What has come to be known as the Deming Cycle illustrates what TQM professionals mean when they talk about a process of continuous quality improvement. After we examine the utility of this approach to the human services, we will explore the central role of teams and teamwork in TQM. I will use the case example of a job-training program to demonstrate the application of TQM tools to the resolution of a quality problem. So what we will be looking at are cycles, teams, and tools.

THE DEMING CYCLE

Many TQM professionals are familiar with what has come to be known as the Deming Cycle (see Figure 7.1). But this takes a certain level of sophistication, and if you are going to be discussing it with some of your colleagues at work, you might be more comfortable in referring to it as the "Plan-Do-Check-Act" cycle.

The Deming Cycle begins with the Plan Stage. At the Plan Stage, a proposal is made to implement a change that hopefully will result in correcting a quality problem, that is, reducing variation in some system or major process. The proposed improvement has not been arrived at by "seat of the pants" guesswork, but rather by the analysis of data to determine the most probable cause of the quality problem and the most likely solution. Many popular American management books extol the virtue of organizations taking immediate and aggressive action when confronted with a problem. For example, Peters and Waterman (1982), in their book *In Search of Excellence*, suggest that organizations and managers should demonstrate a bias for action. According to Peters and Waterman, doing something—even if it is wrong—is preferable to doing nothing. TQM takes exactly the opposite view. According to TQM theory, doing nothing is preferable to doing the wrong thing. A system or process should not be changed unless data have identified the most probable cause of the quality problem. To do otherwise is to run the risk of chasing after the symptoms of quality problems rather than their actual causes.

The Do Stage is the actual controlled experimental portion of the Deming Cycle. The proposed change is implemented while holding constant all other aspects of the system or process. At the Check Stage, the results of the change are evaluated. Did quality improve? Was variation reduced? At the Act Stage, the change—if successful in improving quality—is made a standard operating procedure. If the change does not improve quality, then it is abandoned, and other probable causes of the quality problem are studied. In either case, the Deming Cycle returns to the Plan Stage, where the process begins all

4. Standardize
    Or Abandon
    the Change

3. Evaluate the
    Change

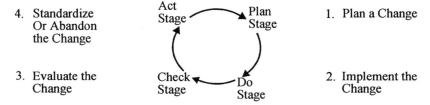

1. Plan a Change

2. Implement the
    Change

Figure 7.1. The Deming Cycle

over again. The Deming Cycle is never completed; there is no end state
to quality or the pursuit of quality improvement.

TEAMS AND TEAMWORK

In understanding how teams and teamwork fit into TQM, a distinction
needs to be made between quality teams and quality circles. Quality
teams look a great deal like quality circles, but they differ considerably
in mission and focus.

QUALITY CIRCLES

The managerial wave known as "quality circles" burst on the American scene in the late 1970s. American management consultants and
educators visiting Japan during the earlier part of the decade observed
that Japanese business firms did everything through teams. Concluding
that this team orientation was the critical variable in the success of
Japanese business firms, these same management consultants and educators returned to the United States and introduced quality circles to
American business, government, and the nonprofit sector.

For the most part, quality circles have not worked well in the United
States (Drucker, 1992, pp. 304-305). The reason most frequently given
for the poor showing of quality circles in the United States is that they
were introduced as stand-alone programs and not as part of larger TQM
programs, as is the case in Japan (Dobyns & Crawford-Mason, 1991;
Juran, 1989; Koons, 1991). Employees working in American quality
circle programs have traditionally been given broad latitude to identify
their own priorities and their own projects. The lack of management
direction has tended to result in a lot of quality circles focusing on
improving the quality of the workplace, rather than on improving the
quality of systems and major processes (Koons, 1991, pp. 37-38). Too

many American quality circle programs wound up becoming employee driven rather than customer driven.

QUALITY TEAMS

A quality team is a group of employees, numbering anywhere from 3 to 12 people (Feigenbaum, 1983, p. 210; Glenn, 1991, p. 19). Quality teams meet at regularly scheduled times, usually a minimum of once a week for at least an hour, to work on agreed-upon (with management) problems designed to improve the quality of systems and major processes (Hutchins, 1985, p. 1). Time spent working on a quality team is considered part of an employee's regular work time. Consequently, most quality teams meet during regularly scheduled working hours. As a general rule, employees are encouraged, but not compelled, to participate on quality teams (Juran, 1989, p. 283).

The membership of a quality team in a human service organization will be largely determined by the nature of the system or process to be improved. For example, if a process is completely internal to one department, then membership on a quality team may well comprise only employees from that department. However, if a whole system (i.e., a program or service) is to be improved, or if a major process has constituent parts that constitute outputs for some departments and inputs for others, then a quality team will probably be composed of both upstream and downstream members.

A suggestion, totally in keeping with the customer driven focus of TQM, but one that has received little attention in the literature, is to include external customers (clients, funding sources, or both) on quality teams (Albrecht, 1992, p. 175). The inclusion of external customers on quality teams should help to ensure that the customer perspective is constantly being considered in team discussions and decision making. Where contractors play an important role in a system or a major process, a quality team would probably also benefit from their participation.

The role of human service managers in quality teams is not to lead, but to be supportive and to ensure that teams stay focused and on-task. Leadership, ideas, and solutions come from team members—those most familiar with a system or major process and its problems—and not from management. When working with quality teams, managers take on the role of coaches. Some essential characteristics of successful quality teams are identified in Table 7.1. Ensuring that quality teams demonstrate these characteristics is the responsibility of management.

TQM does not require that every employee in a human service organization be a member of a quality team, or that quality teams be

TABLE 7.1 Essential Characteristics of Successful Quality Teams

- Have focus
  Systems and processes are selected jointly by management and employees. Quality teams stay on task.

- Have the right members
  Team members represent the systems and processes involved and the skills needed to improve them.

- Have time to work
  Sufficient time is provided to study the process or system, to determine the nature of quality problems, and to implement the most probable solution(s).

- Have teamwork as a priority
  Members of quality teams are committed to working as a team and not as individuals.

- Have excellent communication
  Quality teams promote good communications between themselves and management.

SOURCE: Adapted from Carr and Littman (1990, p. 106).

working simultaneously to improve all the organization's systems and major processes. A general rule of thumb is that a human service organization that has 10% of its employees working on quality teams at any one time is off to a good start. And any human service organization that has more than 60% of its employees working on quality teams at any one time is doing well (Glenn, 1991, p. 19).

THE TOOLS OF TQM

A number of statistical and analytical TQM tools are available for use by human service organizations pursuing continuous quality improvement. Some of the more important tools (such as customer satisfaction surveys, flow charts, and process control charts) have already been discussed. In the following sections four other major TQM tools are discussed: (a) brainstorming, (b) cause-and-effect diagrams, (c) check sheets, and (d) Pareto analysis. These four major TQM tools are used in the Plan Stage of the Deming Cycle, where the potential causes of a quality problem are studied, and the most probable cause, or causes, identified. The use of these TQM tools presupposes that a quality problem has already been identified by using one or more of the approaches discussed in the preceding chapters.

BRAINSTORMING

In brainstorming, the emphasis is on generating as many ideas as possible about the causes of a quality problem. Picture a quality team seated around a table, throwing out ideas—creative, even wild ideas—about the causes of a quality problem so that the broadest perspective possible is brought to bear on the quality problem. Possible causes can be generated in a round-robin fashion, with each quality team member contributing one idea at a time, or any member can offer an idea at any time in a freewheeling fashion.

The ideas generated during a brainstorming session are not critiqued or evaluated. The desired outcome of a brainstorming session is numerous ideas that represent possible causes of the identified quality problem. A few guidelines for use in conducting brainstorming sessions are presented in Table 7.2.

Let us assume that a county human service organization is contracting with a number of nonprofit community-based agencies to provide job-training services under the federal Job Training Partnership Act (JTPA) program. The county human service organization is experiencing a quality problem in reimbursing its JTPA contractors in a timely fashion. This quality problem is having a direct effect on client customers because contractor cash flow problems are, in turn, causing delays and disruptions in the job-training services clients receive. This type of quality problem is referred to as a *cycle time* problem, meaning that the amount of time to accomplish some task needs to be reduced. Cycle time quality problems are prevalent in many of the programs, services, and activities carried out by human service organizations, for example, the processing of food stamp and AFDC applications, the delivery of hot home-delivered meals, the completion of adoption studies, the investigation of child abuse complaints, and others.

The county human service organization decides to convene a quality team to study the problem of late JTPA contractor payments and to formulate a quality improvement strategy. The processing of JTPA contractor payments involves several departments within the organization. Consequently, the quality team contains members from all affected (upstream and downstream) departments.

At the first meeting of the quality team, management goes over the assignment with team members, so that they understand the nature of the quality problem, its importance, and the scope of their assignment. A brainstorming session is then conducted. Several potential reasons or causes, for why JTPA contractor payments are late, are identified and recorded.

TABLE 7.2 Guidelines for Conducting Brainstorming Sessions

1. The goal is to generate as many ideas as possible.
2. All members are encouraged to participate.
3. One idea at a time is presented.
4. All ideas are recorded.
5. No criticism or evaluation of ideas is permitted.

At the next meeting, the quality team decides to categorize and evaluate the potential causes, using a cause-and-effect diagram.

CAUSE-AND-EFFECT DIAGRAMS

Cause-and-effect diagrams are used to organize and evaluate the ideas, the potential causes of quality problems, identified during brainstorming sessions. A basic cause-and-effect diagram is shown in Figure 7.2. Cause-and-effect diagrams are also known as fishbone charts because of their similarity to the skeletal structure of fish.

The effect, or the quality problem, is listed on the right side of the cause-and-effect diagram, and all the possible causes developed from the brainstorming session are on the left. The use of predetermined categories to organize and evaluate the various potential causes is sometimes helpful. Two common classification schemas are the "4Ms" (methods, manpower, machinery, and materials) and the "4Ps" (people, policies, procedures, and plant). The "4Ps" classification schema is considered more appropriate for use in studying quality problems of a service or administrative nature, while the "4Ms" are considered more appropriate for use in studying quality problems of a manufacturing or production nature (Brassard, 1988, p. 24). These categories are only suggestions, and quality teams are free to develop their own classification schemas.

In addition to helping organize the various potential causes of a quality problem into a more manageable number of categories, the cause-and-effect diagram also shows the interrelationships between potential causes. A visual display of these interrelationships can frequently help simplify the analysis, by highlighting one or two of the categories while downplaying the others. For example, if the overwhelming majority of potential causes of a quality problem fall into the categories of "policies" and "procedures," the subsequent analysis can probably focus on these areas, while the categories of "people" and "plant" can probably be set aside. Using the cause-and-effect diagram

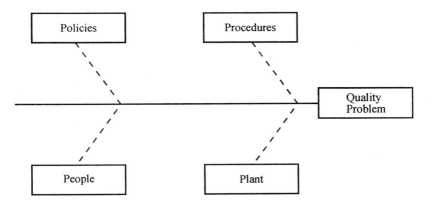

Figure 7.2. A Basic Cause-and-Effect Diagram

as the basis for discussion, quality teams continue to analyze and evaluate the various potential causes of a quality problem until consensus is achieved concerning a smaller number of most probable causes.

Returning to the example of the county human service organization and late payments to JTPA contractors, let us assume that at the second meeting of the quality team, the cause-and-effect diagram shown in Figure 7.3 was completed. Using the cause-and-effect diagram as a basis for discussion, the quality team members evaluate all potential causes and arrive at a consensus that the three most probable causes of late JTPA contractor payments are (a) contractors submitting invoices late, (b) contractors submitting incomplete or incorrect invoices, or (c) excessive processing time—the county human service organization taking more than 30 days to process the invoices.

Before the next meeting, two quality team members agree to collect data on the frequency of the three identified most probable causes and report back to the full committee.

CHECK SHEETS

Check sheets are used by quality teams to collect data on the causes of quality problems. A check sheet is simply a count, or frequency distribution, of the number of times a potential cause of a quality problem was detected or observed.

Returning again to the case example of the late JTPA contractor payments, let us assume that the two quality team members identify 25 instances where JTPA contractors were paid late during the past 120

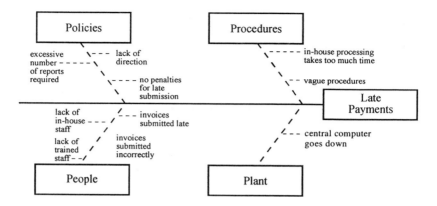

Figure 7.3. A Completed Cause-and-Effect Diagram for Late JTPA Contractor Payments

days. For each such occurrence, they determine if the cause was either one of the three most probable causes or another cause. Table 7.3 shows the check sheet data.

PARETO ANALYSIS

Pareto analysis is a method of breaking a quality problem down into its constituent parts and ordering the parts, according to their frequency or magnitude (Motorola, 1992). A Pareto chart has two major purposes. One is to identify those "important few" causes that make the largest contribution to a quality problem. The second is to represent the data visually, which facilitates understanding the quality problem. The data needed to construct a Pareto chart can generally be taken directly from a check sheet.

Figure 7.4 shows a Pareto chart for the late JTPA contractor payments developed from the check sheet data in Table 7.3. The vertical scale of a Pareto chart is usually the total number of defects contributing to a quality problem—in this case, the total number of late JTPA contractor payments. The types of defects (the causes of the late JTPA contractor payments, in this case) are usually arranged horizontally, in descending order along the bottom of the chart. The resulting Pareto chart provides a visual perspective of the most frequent causes of a quality problem and permits order of magnitude comparisons between causes.

As Figure 7.4 illustrates, excessive processing time on the part of the county human service organization is the most frequent cause of late

TABLE 7.3 Check Sheet and Data for Causes of Late JTPA Contractor Payments

Most Probable Causes	Frequency
Invoices late	7
Invoices incorrect	0
Excessive in-house processing time	15
Other causes	3
Total observations	25

JTPA contractor payments. Fifteen of the 25 late JTPA contractor payments are attributable to excessive processing time. The next most frequent cause is JTPA contractors submitting their invoices late. Seven late payments are attributable to this cause. A relatively unimportant "other" category accounts for the remaining 3 late JPTA contractor payments.

At the next weekly meeting of the quality team, the Pareto chart is discussed, and the team members agree that the appropriate quality improvement strategy is to work on finding ways to reduce the cycle time it takes the county human service organization to process JTPA contractor payments.

IMPROVING SYSTEMS AND MAJOR PROCESSES

Once the cause of a quality problem in a system or major process is determined, the next step is to devise a quality improvement strategy. As Table 7.4 points out, there are three basic quality improvement strategies.

Doing it better refers to making an existing system or major process function with fewer mistakes and less duplication. For example, doing it better might involve reducing the number of people or steps involved (and thus decreasing the opportunity for mistakes to occur), or changing a sequential flow to a parallel flow or vice versa. Doing it differently requires that the system or major process be reconceptualized or redesigned. Doing without it refers to finding ways to eliminate the system or major process altogether.

In the case example of late JTPA contractors, doing without it will not work as a quality improvement strategy because contractors must be paid. Doing it better will also not work because there are no errors per se to correct. Thus the appropriate quality improvement strategy for

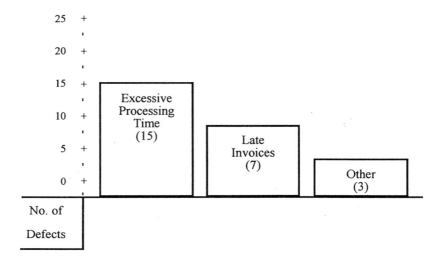

Figure 7.4. A Pareto Chart for Late JTPA Contractor Payments

late JTPA contractor payments is to do it differently. In point of fact, most cycle time quality problems involve doing it differently.

Let us assume that the quality team constructs a flow chart of the JPTA contractor payment system and discovers that a number of people in the county human service organization must review and approve each invoice. The quality team decides to redesign the system so that all secondary reviews and approvals are removed. From now on only one person will review and approve each JPTA contractor payment. However, at the end of each month, a supervisor will audit a sample of JPTA contractor payments to check for errors, overpayments, and underpayments. By removing all the redundant reviews and approvals, the quality team computes that the average cycle time to process a JPTA contractor payment can be reduced from the current 37 days to fewer than 25 days.

At the next meeting of the quality team, a formal presentation is made to management on the quality problem with late JPTA contractor payments. The quality team presents the system flow chart, the cause-and-effect diagram, the check sheet, and the Pareto chart. After listening to the presentation and reviewing the data, management agrees with the findings and conclusions of the quality team and suggests that the proposed changes be instituted as soon as possible.

TABLE 7.4 Three Major Quality Improvement Strategies

1. Do it better.
2. Do it differently.
3. Do without it.

SOURCE: Albrecht (1992, pp. 162-163).

The quality team meets again the following week and turns its attention to the second most frequent cause of late JPTA contractor payments—incorrect or incomplete invoices. The quality team begins brainstorming possible causes for this quality problem, and thus the Deming Cycle begins all over again.

Chapter 8

TOP MANAGEMENT COMMITMENT

The importance of top management support is essential to the success of any new managerial initiative (Gummesson, 1991; Rogers & Hunter, 1992). In the case of TQM, the unqualified commitment of top management is absolutely essential. On this point all four of the major American quality experts (Deming, Crosby, Juran, and Feigenbaum) agree. Unfortunately, many TQM efforts demonstrate some initial success and then fizzle out because top management support wanes (*Business Week*, 1991; Zeithaml et al., 1990).

To ensure the success of TQM in a human service organization, top management must be committed to (a) creating a culture of quality, (b) maintaining a long-term perspective, and (c) empowering employees.

CREATING A CULTURE OF QUALITY

The term *organizational culture* is a recent addition to the management lexicon. Organizational culture can be defined as the basic values and norms that underlie how organizations operate (Alvesson & Berg, 1992, p. 77). As suggested in Chapter 1, the basic values and norms that underlie most American organizations are those of individualism, entrepreneuralism, competition, "gut level" decision making, top-down communication, and others. The primary task for top human service managers working in a TQM environment is to transform the existing organizational culture to one based on the values and norms of TQM. This transformation includes a shift to customer defined quality, the primacy of teams and teamwork, the empowerment of employees, an emphasis on cooperation rather than competition, a preference for two-way communication, and a focus on structured scientific/analytical decision making.

How can top managers of human service organizations go about transforming their organizational cultures? No hard-and-fast rules exist, but the basic notion is that top management must provide leadership in both (a) setting the *tone* for change and (b) taking specific key actions designed to facilitate the transformation. According to Peters and Austin (1985, p. 285), in order to accomplish these two leadership tasks, top management must have vision, dramatize the desired results, and act as chief salesman for the new organizational culture of TQM.

SETTING THE TONE

Setting the tone for change and the transformation to TQM frequently involves the use of themes, slogans, and symbols, which are repeated so often that they essentially become part of the organizational psyche. The challenge here is for top management not just to be personally committed to change, but also to overtly—and continuously—demonstrate and communicate the depth of that commitment to the organization at large. Top managers can believe in something but fail to communicate that commitment to others in the organization and thereby inspire them. The employees of a human service organization must know, and must be convinced, that top management is committed to a transformation to a TQM organizational culture.

One example of using a dramatic action to set the tone for change in an organization was related to the author by a top manager of a Fortune 500 company that is also a winner of the Baldrige Award. The president of the company, after becoming personally committed to TQM and the transformation of the existing organizational culture, sent a none too subtle message to the organization at large by simply refusing to concern himself with any other matters. For example, at staff meetings, the implementation of TQM was made the first order of business. When the various operating divisions had made their TQM reports, the president turned the meeting over to a subordinate and promptly left the room. The president's actions quickly became a part of the "folklore" of the company's new TQM organizational culture.

An example of the use of slogans and symbols is provided by the Maricopa County (Phoenix, Arizona) Department of Social Services (MCDOSS). When MCDOSS decided to implement a TQM program, one of the first actions taken by top management was to develop vision, mission, and value statements reflecting the values and norms of the new organizational culture (see Table 8.1). The value statements stress quality, employee empowerment, and teamwork, while the vision statement even sets a time frame, January 1, 1994, for MCDOSS to become nationally recognized as a leader in the provision of quality social services. The constant repetition of "We" in the vision, mission, and value statements is premeditated and is designed to stress the importance of cooperation, teams, and teamwork in the new organizational culture of TQM. The MCDOSS vision, mission, and value statements can be found prominently displayed in offices, meeting rooms, and hallways of the organization's facilities.

Another example of the use of slogans and visual reinforcers used by MCDOSS is the logo shown in Figure 8.1. The logo again stresses key aspects of the new organizational culture: vision, common objectives, cooperation, and teamwork. Like the vision, mission, and values statement, the MCDOSS logo can be found prominently displayed throughout MCDOSS facilities. The logo also appears on wall and pocket calendars. The MCDOSS logo was developed by an employee as part of an organization-wide contest.

KEY ACTIONS

While dramatic actions, slogans, and symbols help to set the tone for change and adoption of TQM values and norms, they cannot do the whole job of changing an organizational culture by themselves. Top management must also engage in more specific actions to actually facilitate the transformation. In other words, top management needs a "game plan" or strategy.

Brian Dumaine identifies (see Table 8.2) several key actions that he believes top managers should follow in attempting to transform an organizational culture to one based on the values and norms of TQM (cited in Perine, 1990, p. 47). First, according to Dumaine, top management should begin by understanding the current organizational culture. By so doing, tactics can be developed to overcome organizational rigidity to change. Second, top management should identify, encourage, and recognize those employees who criticized and challenged the old organizational culture in the past, because they are the ones most likely to become trailblazers in accepting the new organizational culture of TQM.

Third, Dumaine cautions that an existing organizational culture should not be attacked head-on. Instead, he suggests that top management should help employees and teams work around, over, and through the existing organizational culture until TQM has taken root and grown to a point where it is strong enough to challenge the old organizational culture head-on. Fourth, Dumaine suggests that top managers should live the TQM culture they are trying to create. Nothing sends a stronger message to an organization at large than when employees see top managers

TABLE 8.1 Maricopa County Department of Social Services Value Statements

Our Vision

By January 1, 1994, *We* will be recognized nationally as a public sector leader in the provision of quality social services.

Our Mission

We foster and promote community and individual self-reliance among the residents of Maricopa County, Arizona.

Our Values

Quality Emphasis

– *We* do the appropriate thing correctly the first time to fulfill our customers'/clients' needs in a cost-effective, efficient, and safe environment.

– *We* focus on problem prevention and quality improvement in our jobs.

– *We* see quality operations as a key to improving our productivity.

– *We* link rewards to quality results.

Employee Involvement

– *We* engage in open, inclusive, and information-based decision making.

– *We* delegate decision making as deep into our organization as possible.

– *We* are all afforded the opportunity to contribute in areas of our expertise.

Teamwork

– *We* use teamwork to develop and foster common objectives throughout our organization.

– *We* believe cooperative relationships, both internally and externally, are essential to our success.

SOURCE: Maricopa County Department of Social Services (1991). Reprinted with permission.

actually practicing what they preach. Finally, Dumaine points out, as does virtually everyone associated with TQM and the quality management movement, that the transformation will not be accomplished overnight.

A LONG-TERM PERSPECTIVE

The time and effort required to change an organizational culture to one based on the values and norms of TQM can be lengthy. One top manager, who was ultimately successful in changing his organizational

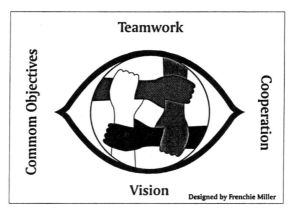

Figure 8.1. Maricopa County Department of Social Services Logo From 1992
Values Calendar*
*Reprinted with permission.

culture to accept TQM values and norms, described the process as being
governed by the rule of threes: It is three times more difficult, takes
three times as long, and costs three times more than you originally
figured (Albrecht, 1992, p. 59).

How long should human service organizations reasonably expect the
transformation process to take? Table 8.3 is Juran's (1989) attempt to
answer this question. According to Juran, a minimum of 5½ years is
required before TQM can be expected to be operating smoothly in most
organizations. The evidence from the American automobile industry
suggests that Juran's timetable is highly accurate. Ford and General
Motors, two of the earliest American companies to adopt TQM programs, did not really see major results until the early 1990s.

The first activity in Juran's timetable is the selection of an implementation strategy. Two major implementation strategies exist: (a) involving the
whole organization at once or (b) adopting a unit-by-unit approach. The
bulk of TQM experience, as well as common sense, suggests that the
unit-by-unit approach is preferable (Carr & Littman, 1990, p. 252). The
major advantage of the unit-by-unit approach is that each unit can find
its own comfort level with TQM. Some evidence also exists to suggest
that the unit-by-unit approach is preferred by middle managers and
employees (Carr & Littman, 1990, p. 252).

TABLE 8.2 Key Actions in Changing an Organizational Culture

1. Understand the existing culture first.
2. Encourage employees who have criticized or attacked the existing culture in the past.
3. Don't attack the existing culture head-on.
4. Live the culture you are trying to create.
5. Understand that the transformation will not occur overnight.

SOURCE: Adapted from Perine (1990, p. 48).

EMPLOYEE EMPOWERMENT

If an organizational culture is to be transformed into one based on the values and norms of TQM, top management must also be committed to employee empowerment. Employee empowerment can be thought of as any effort designed to move power, information, knowledge, and rewards downward in the organization (*Business Week*, 1992, p. 47). The premise on which employee empowerment rests is a belief in the creative energies of the people who really understand an organization's systems and major processes.

Several of Deming's 14 points (see Chapter 2) are designed to empower employees. As a general rule, Deming recommends removing all barriers that rob employees of pride and ownership in their work. He also specifically advocates a vigorous program of employee training and self-improvement. An interesting caveat concerning employee training is that evaluations of TQM programs suggest that employees must be provided with detailed training and instruction in how to do their jobs better from a TQM perspective, because most employees believe they are already doing the best job possible (Koons, 1991, p. 35).

In addition to the basic quality teams approach detailed in Chapter 7, other interesting examples of employee empowerment approaches are provided by Wal-Mart, Walt Disney World in Orlando, Florida, Motorola, and General Mills. At Wal-Mart, the large retail chain, knowledge is pushed down through the organization through the provision of scholarships that enable employees to complete their educations. Some 40% of Wal-Mart managers started with the company as hourly workers. At Walt Disney World, power is pushed downward in the organization by a unique program that encourages employees to recruit new employees. This program is again based on the belief that the people actually

TABLE 8.3 Juran's Timetable for Implementing TQM

Phase	Time Required
1. Selection of implementation strategy	6-12 months
2. Test site implementation and evaluation	1 year
3. Scaling up for TQM organization-wide	2 years
4. Complete implementation of TQM, including tools	2 years
Total time	5.5-6 years

SOURCE: Adapted from Juran (1989, p. 215).

performing the work are the ones most qualified to recruit and hire new employees (Zeithaml et al., 1990, p. 166).

At Motorola, rewards are pushed downward in the organization. Quality teams that make significant strides in quality improvement are recognized by top management and rewarded with vacation trips to such places as Hawaii. Quality teams are drawn from all parts of the company and include both white- and blue-collar employees. The General Mills Company may have one of the most aggressive employee empowerment programs. At several General Mills plants, power, information, knowledge, and rewards have all been pushed downward in the organization, through the creation of 20-person employee teams that actually run the plants and handle most aspects of production, marketing, and sales (*Business Week*, 1992, p. 50).

ORGANIZATIONAL GOAL DISPLACEMENT IN TQM

In addition to the responsibilities described above, top human service managers attempting to transform an organizational culture to one based on TQM norms and values have at least one additional major job responsibility, ensuring that organizational goal displacement does not occur. Organizational goal displacement can take many forms, but some of the more common forms appear to be (a) losing sight of the customer, (b) falling prey to the measure and improve fallacy, and (c) quality being everyone's job and consequently being no one's job.

LOSING SIGHT OF THE CUSTOMER

A problem that can occur in organizations rushing to implement TQM is that the customer simply gets lost. I once interviewed several staff members of a large health organization that was just beginning to implement a TQM program. I was provided with a long and detailed briefing about the organization's approach to TQM. During the briefing, it became obvious that something important was missing. No mention was made of the organization's customers or their quality preferences. At the end of the briefing, I asked the question: "What about the customers?" The response I got was that the implementation of TQM was too high a priority for the organization to wait until customer attitudes and preferences could be assessed. The staff did assure me, however, that after the TQM program was up and running, allowances would be made for customer input.

This anecdote is a prime example of organizational goal displacement by losing sight of the customer. The organization had become so caught up in the trappings, paperwork, and terminology of TQM that it lost sight of the true meaning and philosophy of TQM. It is impossible to have a TQM program without a customer focus.

THE MEASURE AND IMPROVE FALLACY

Another form of organizational goal displacement in TQM is the measure and improve fallacy. Any system or process in an organization can be measured and improved. An organization can become so caught up in measuring and improving everything in sight that the whole process winds up imploding in a mass of paperwork. This is precisely what happened to Florida Power & Light, a public utility and the first American company to win the Deming quality award. Florida Power & Light became so caught up in the paperwork, slogans, and trappings of TQM—to say nothing of the time and energy required to prepare for the Deming competition—that the organization's business actually suffered (*Business Week*, 1991, pp. 34-38).

What prevents an organization from falling victim to the measure and improve fallacy is a customer focus. If customer quality data suggest that a particular system or process is relatively unimportant, then it should not be targeted for measurement and improvement until all other quality critical systems and major processes have first been addressed.

QUALITY AS EVERYBODY'S AND NOBODY'S JOB

Yet another form of organizational goal displacement can occur when quality becomes a part of everyone's job. Feigenbaum (1983, p. 158) has stated the nature of the problem thus, "because quality is part of everyone's job, . . . it may become nobody's." Feigenbaum is suggesting that even though quality may become a part of everyone's job in a TQM

TABLE 8.4 Responsibilities of Quality Councils

---

1. Formulate TQM policy for the organization.
2. Establish criteria for TQM project/team selection.
3. Ensure resources are provided to TQM projects/teams.
4. Monitor the progress of TQM projects/teams to ensure successful completion.
5. Make provision for appropriate TQM project/team group recognition and rewards.

SOURCE: Adapted from Juran (1989, p. 45).

environment, some sort of organizational mechanism is still needed to oversee and coordinate the effort.

Juran (1989) maintains that the appropriate mechanism to oversee and coordinate the implementation of TQM in an organization is a quality council. The membership on a quality council is comprised of top management. As Table 8.4 illustrates, the major purpose of a quality council is to bring focus to TQM efforts by ensuring that projects/teams operate within acceptable organizational parameters. The Federal Quality Institute (FQI) is an example of a quality council. The FQI oversees and coordinates TQM efforts in the various departments and branches of the federal government.

Chapter 9

CONTRACTOR INVOLVEMENT

Phil Crosby (1980, p. 61) has observed that most American companies spend about 50% of their income on vendor or contractor products and services. One of the implications of this finding is that most American companies do not have total control over the quality of their own products and services. Most American companies represent downstream users relying on a number of upstream supplier contractors. If the products and services provided by these upstream suppliers are not of a high quality, then the products and services of the company cannot be of a high quality. Consequently, Crosby, as well as the other three major American quality experts (Deming, Juran, and Feigenbaum), all agree that upstream supplier contractors must be included if the TQM programs of American companies are to be successful.

The Japanese have understood the quality implications of supplier/user relationships for some time; American companies have only recently come to understand the nature of this quality interdependency. American businesses like Motorola, Ford, and Xerox have all moved to reduce the number of upstream supplier contractors they deal with. In deciding which ones to keep and which ones to let go, quality is the determining factor. The upstream suppliers that are kept tend to become full partners in the TQM programs of the companies they supply.

Human service organizations closely parallel American companies in their degree of quality interdependency with contractors. During the decade of the 1970s, a quiet revolution took place in the human services. Purchase of service contracting (POSC) between government and private human service organizations, both nonprofit and for-profit, became the major mode of delivering publicly funded human services in this country (Benton, Field, & Millar, 1978; Kettner & Martin, 1987; Mueller, 1980).

Today many private human service organizations derive upwards of 60% or more of their total revenues from POSC (Terrell, 1987). Thus, government and private human service organizations are as mutually interdependent as are American companies and their contractors. In the human services, however, the direction of the relationship is reversed. Government human service organizations are upstream in the process flow, while private human service contractors are downstream.

This upstream government and downstream private contractor interdependency creates some interesting quality issues when attempts are made to combine TQM with POSC. Government human service organizations cannot control the ultimate quality of their products and services, unless they can exercise at least some control over the systems and major processes of downstream private human service contractors. Conversely, downstream private contractors do not have total control over the quality of the products and services they provide, because their actions are circumscribed by a host of contractual requirements and obligations placed on them by upstream government human service organizations. In other words, the quality of the products and services received by government customer clients today depends to a great extent on how well government and private human service organizations manage their POSC interdependencies.

This chapter explores the quality implications of POSC interdependencies in three areas. First, the quality implications of using design and performance specifications in POSC work statements are discussed. Next, the quality implications of different government procurement systems are explored. Last, the adoption of a partnership model of POSC is suggested as a method of promoting long-term, quality-based POSC relationships.

THE QUALITY IMPLICATIONS OF DESIGN AND PERFORMANCE SPECIFICATIONS

All POSC contracts contain a section known as the work statement, statement of work, service specifications, or some such similar designation. The term *work statement* is used here. When developing work statements, government human service contracting agencies can choose to use design specifications, performance specifications, or a combination.

Design specifications can be defined as the framework or structure within which the contracted product is to be produced or the contracted service is to be provided. Design specifications establish specific dimensions, tolerances, workmanship, and other measures of a quality nature for a system and its major processes. *Performance specifications* can be defined as the criteria by which the results or outcomes (also a quality dimension) of product production or service provision are to be evaluated.

As these two definitions suggest, ensuring quality in POSC products and services requires the use of both design and performance specifications in work statements. Design specifications are used to establish and operationally define such quality dimensions as reliability, accessibility, assurance, empathy, and tangibles. Performance specifications are used to establish and operationally define results or outcomes—what happened to client customers as a result of product production and service provision.

As discussed in Chapter 6, a basic tenet of TQM is that quality suffers when too much variation occurs in systems and major processes. Translated to POSC, variation occurs in product production and service provision when government human service organizations use inadequate, ambiguous, or poorly developed design or performance specifications in their work statements. In order for a government human service organization to minimize variation in a contract product or service, private human service contractors should have minimal discretion over how a product is produced or how a service is provided (design specifications) or the expected results or outcomes (performance specifications).

Let us assume for the sake of illustration that a government human service contracting agency decides to use POSC for case management services. A case management system is designed and flow charted. The case management system has eight major processes (see Table 9.1). Design specifications could then be developed, detailing exactly how each of the major processes is to be carried out. The design specifications could then be included in a work statement for case management services. Formulated in this manner, the design specifications and work statement should ensure that all private human service contractors perform each of the major processes in essentially the same way. This standardized approach should, in turn, ensure that each client customer receives essentially the same type of product or service (reliability). As a result of standardization, (a) variation in product production or service provision between client customers should be minimal, (b) overall product or service quality should be high, and (c) customer satisfaction levels should also be high.

Quality indicators for each of the eight major processes in the case management system could also be constructed and incorporated as design specifications in a work statement. The quality indicators could then be monitored and tracked by both the private human service contractor and the government human service organization.

TABLE 9.1   Major Processes in a Case Management System

---
1. Intake and screening of a client customer
2. Problem identification and assessment
3. Case planning
4. Implementation of the case plan
5. Monitoring of the case plan
6. Evaluation of effects of service delivery on a client customer
7. Termination of a client customer from service
8. Follow-up as needed

SOURCE: Kettner, Moroney, and Martin (1990, p. 116).

Although design specifications can be used to ensure that variation on such quality dimensions as reliability, accessibility, assurance, empathy, and tangibles is minimized, performance specifications are needed to define, measure, and control variation in results or outcomes. Kettner, Moroney, and Martin (1990, pp. 119-122) identify four types of outcome measures that can be used as the basis for developing performance specifications: (a) *numeric counts*, or the number of client customers who successfully complete their service plan or receive a full complement of services; (b) *standardized measures*, such as the MMPI (Minnesota Multiphasic Personality Inventory) and the ADL (Activities of Daily Living) scales, which measure a client customer's progress or status on a generally accepted scale; (c) *level of functioning scales*, which are similar to standardized measures, but differ in that they are program or agency specific; and (d) *client customer satisfaction*.

Reducing variation in POSC products and services begins with the use of design and performance specifications in work statements. Continuous quality improvement, however, requires that government human service organizations collect data on the relative influence, or effect, of various design specifications on performance specifications in an ongoing "Deming Wheel" controlled experiment. Using the results, or outcomes, of product production and service provision as the dependent variable, changes (improvements) in various design specifications (the independent variables) can be made in a controlled fashion, in an attempt to arrive at the optimum mix of design specifications to achieve the greatest results or best outcomes, as measured by performance specifications.

Perhaps the best way to ensure the optimum mix of design specifications in a work statement is for government human service organizations to include private contractors on quality teams for all contracted products and services. When serving on quality teams, private human service contractors should be treated as full partners.

THE QUALITY IMPLICATIONS
OF GOVERNMENT PROCUREMENT SYSTEMS

Government procurement systems can either promote or retard quality in POSC. As Figure 9.1 demonstrates, government procurement systems are of three basic types: (a) formal advertising, (b) competitive negotiation, and (c) the two-step method (Kettner & Martin, 1987, p. 78).

In formal advertising, also known by such names as bidding, sealed bidding, and competitive sealed bidding, the major decision criterion in contract award is price or cost. In competitive negotiation, more commonly known as the RFP process, the major decision criteria are cost and other factors (e.g., quality) (Kettner & Martin, 1987). In the two-step process, technical proposals are solicited at Step 1. At Step 2, all proposers whose technical proposals are considered acceptable (that satisfy all quality standards) are then permitted to bid. The contract is awarded on the basis of the most advantageous price or cost.

Formal competition clearly has detrimental implications for quality in POSC. As was pointed out in Chapter 1, when a focus is placed on cost, rather than on quality, productivity actually suffers. Every government human service organization has at least one major horror story about a POSC contract awarded to a low bidder that was a disaster for the agency and for client customers.

As an alternative to formal advertising, many government human service organizations prefer to use competitive negotiation, or the RFP process. In the RFP process, price is only one of several potential decision factors, or criteria, used in making contracting decisions. Competitive negotiation is clearly superior to formal advertising, because quality is considered in contract award. Nevertheless, competitive negotiation is still less than optimal in promoting quality in POSC, because a weight of as much as 50% is still frequently given to price or cost.

The only procurement system that actually puts quality first in POSC is the two-step process. When people first hear about two-step procurement, they immediately think this approach must be inordinately complicated because it combines both formal advertising and competitive negotiation into one process. In actuality, the conducting of a two-step procurement is no more complicated and need not take any longer than either of the other two procurement systems. The way in which many two-step systems work is that prospective contractors submit two sealed

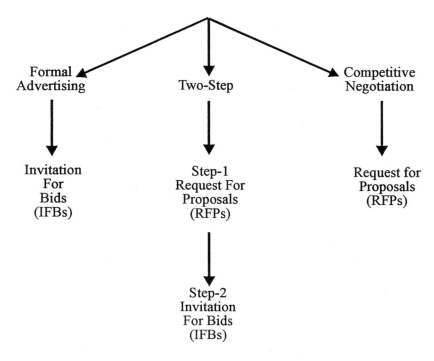

Figure 9.1. Government Procurement Systems Formal Advertising

envelopes. One envelope contains the technical proposal; the other contains price and cost information.

At Step 1, only the envelopes containing the technical proposals are opened. The envelopes containing the price or cost data are kept sealed. Again, only those proposers submitting acceptable technical proposals, including agreeing to meet all work statement design and performance specifications, advance to Step 2. At Step 2, the second envelopes are opened, and the contract is awarded to the prospective contractor whose price or cost is most advantageous to the government human service organization.

What the two-step procurement does that the other two procurement systems do not, is to ensure that quality in product production and service provision is given top priority before any consideration is given to cost or price. It is impossible for a prospective contractor proposing a low-quality product or service to be the low bidder or proposer, because they are screened out at Step 1. The two-step process is legal in most states and is frequently considered an acceptable substitute when a particular product or service is required to be contracted using formal advertising (Council of State Governments, 1983).

THE PARTNERSHIP MODEL OF POSC

Many human service administrators erroneously believe that competition must be maximized when using POSC. This belief is incorrect and may be retarding the development of positive long-term relationships between the public and private human service sectors using POSC and quality as the linking mechanisms.

Kettner and Martin (1986, 1987) conceptualize two approaches to POSC: (a) the market model, and (b) the partnership model. The *market model* is defined as a set of policies and practices on the part of government human service organizations that encourages competition between prospective contractors, and where like contractors are competing to provide a like product or service, price is the primary decision criterion (Kettner & Martin, 1987, p. 35). The *partnership model* of POSC is defined as a set of policies and practices on the part of government human service organizations that view government and the private sector as two parts of a comprehensive and interdependent human services system (Kettner & Martin, 1987, p. 32).

The partnership model of POSC is a way of translating into action Deming's (1986, p. 4), admonition that vendors or contractors should be made formal partners in TQM programs. Using the partnership model of POSC, in conjunction with properly constructed design and performance specifications and two-step procurement, government human service organizations can further their TQM programs and develop long-term quality relationships with contractors.

Several POSC administrative mechanisms can be identified as being either more or less compatible with the partnership model or market models and, by extension, either promote or retard an emphasis on quality. These POSC administrative mechanisms are identified in Table 9.2.

Multiyear contracts are considered more compatible with the partnership model and with TQM, because when a government human service organization finds a private human service contractor that will make quality a top priority, the POSC relationship can be "locked in" for the long term. Single-year POSC contracts, on the other hand, require that a procurement process be conducted each year, which, in turn, simply increases the probability of a nonquality conscious contractor receiving a contract.

TABLE 9.2   Administrative Mechanism and the Partnership/Market Models of POSC

More Characteristic of the Market Model	*More Characteristic of the Partnership Model*
• Single-year contracts • Unit cost, fixed-fee, and incentive contracts • Government, nonprofit, and for-profit contractors	• Multiyear contracts • Cost reimbursement contracts • Government and nonprofit contractors

SOURCE: Adapted from Kettner and Martin (1986).

Cost reimbursement contracts are also considered more compatible with the partnership model of POSC and TQM because a contractor's full costs are defrayed. When cost or price is a major consideration, as is the case in the use of unit cost, fixed-fee, and incentive contracts, contractors may be inclined to sacrifice quality to cut costs. An exception to this general statement would be if quality improvement is made the basis for an incentive contract. Finally, the use of government and nonprofit contractors is considered more compatible with the partnership model and TQM because these types of contractors do not have bottom-line profit considerations to take into account.

Chapter 10

A PLAN FOR IMPLEMENTING TQM

Now that we have explored both the philosophy and the tools of TQM, let us discuss how a human service organization might actually go about implementing TQM. While the preceding chapters have already shed a great deal of light on this subject, we have not yet pulled everything together into a "how-to" implementation plan.

Before proceeding with this task, however, a disclaimer is in order. The point was made earlier in this book that it is probably impossible to develop a definitive TQM cookbook. This point is worth stressing one more time. There is no one best way to implement TQM. The organizational setting, the level of commitment of top and middle management, the education and training levels of staff, these factors and others necessarily shape the optimum TQM implementation plan for any particular human service organization. Nevertheless, it is possible to set out a basic plan for implementing TQM, provided we remember that this plan is simply *one* approach and not the *only* approach. The best use a human service organization can probably make of this plan is to adapt it, rather than adopt it. Table 10.1 presents the TQM implementation plan in outline form.

TRAINING TOP MANAGEMENT

The implementation plan begins with top management of the human service organization (the director and division or unit heads) being exposed to an in-depth seminar or workshop on TQM. The seminar or workshop should include both the philosophy and the tools of TQM, but with more stress being placed on the philosophy. This early exposure

TABLE 10.1 A Plan for Implementing TQM in a Human Service Organization

---

   I. Training Top Management

      A. The philosophy of TQM

      B. The tools of TQM

  II. Soliciting Top Management Commitment

      A. The director and top management personally commit to the philosophy of TQM.

      B. The director and top management communicate this commitment to middle managers and front-line staff via:

         1. issuing a policy directive on TQM

         2. making TQM an agenda item for all staff meetings

         3. creating a quality council

 III. Forming the Quality Council

      A. The composition of the quality council is the director and top management.

      B. The purpose of the quality council is to:

         1. bring focus to the TQM effort

         2. coordinate all TQM activities

         3. approve the creation and monitor the activities of quality teams

 IV. Selecting the Implementation Strategy

      The quality council selects either:

      A. The cascading strategy

         1. the whole organization becomes involved with TQM simultaneously

         2. training and involvement with TQM is to flow from the top down, through the middle managers to staff in a cascading fashion

      B. The unit-by-unit strategy:

         1. an incremental approach is taken

         2. one division or unit is selected to be a demonstration

         3. the lessons learned from the demonstration unit are then transferred to other units

---

to TQM is necessary to ensure that top management knows exactly what it and the organization will be getting into.

A large number of organizations and individuals, including many universities and community colleges, are available to conduct seminars and workshops on TQM.

SOLICITING TOP MANAGEMENT COMMITMENT

Once top management has been exposed to the realities of TQM through a seminar or workshop, the next step is for top management to

TABLE 10.1 Continued

V. Training of Middle Managers and Staff

    A. The philosophy of TQM

    B. The use of quality teams

    C. The collection and interpretation of customer quality data

    D. The use of process control charts, brainstorming, cause-and-effect diagrams, check sheets, and Pareto Analysis

VI. Collecting and Analyzing Customer Quality Data

    A. Focus groups are used to determine the quality dimension preferences of customers.

    B. Systems are established to routinely collect customer quality data.

VII. Forming Quality Teams

    A. Staff form quality teams and identify quality problems to be worked on.

    B. The quality council reviews and approves or modifies the composition of quality teams and/or the quality problems to be worked on.

VIII. Recognizing Superior Quality Improvement.

    A. The quality council establishes group incentives for significant quality improvements.

    B. Incentives can take the form of cash awards, gain-sharing awards, trips, release time, and other forms of group recognition.

IX. Continuous Quality Improvement

    A. Once a quality team has resolved a quality problem, it tackles another problem, or disbands and the members join new quality teams.

    B The process continues in the never ending quest for continuous quality improvement.

make a commitment to TQM. This commitment implies not only the personal commitment of the director and division or unit heads, but also the ongoing communication of this commitment to middle management and staff.

Concrete actions that the director and top management can take to demonstrate their commitment to TQM are (a) to issue a policy directive concerning TQM, (b) to make TQM an item of discussion at all staff meetings, and (c) to create a quality council.

FORMING THE QUALITY COUNCIL

An important step in implementing TQM in a human service organization is the formation of a quality council. A quality council is usually composed of the director and top managers. In smaller human service organizations, the quality council might include, or be totally composed of, program managers. The purpose of the quality council is to bring focus to and coordinate all TQM activities, including oversight of quality teams. Minutes of the meetings of the quality council should be kept and disseminated, so that middle managers and staff can have the most up-to-date information on the progress of TQM implementation in the organization.

The continued high-profile involvement of the director with the quality council is essential because it sends a reinforcing message to the organization: TQM is important.

SELECTING THE IMPLEMENTATION STRATEGY

At some point the director and the quality council must decide on an implementation strategy. Two major strategies exist: (a) the cascading strategy and (b) the unit-by-unit strategy. The *cascading strategy* focuses on the entire organization, beginning with top management and cascading downward through the organization to middle managers and then to staff.

The *unit-by-unit strategy* is an incremental approach. One department or unit is initially selected as a demonstration site for TQM. The department or unit selected is frequently the one where middle managers and staff exhibit the greatest support for TQM. The implementation lessons learned from the demonstration are then transferred to other units as they are brought on-line with TQM.

TRAINING OF MIDDLE MANAGERS AND STAFF

At some point, the quality council must necessarily arrange for middle management and staff training in the philosophy and the tools of TQM. The implementation strategy selected (cascading or unit-by-unit) will largely determine who attends training, and when. In either case, middle managers should be trained before staff. This approach enables middle managers to be immediately available to assume their roles as coaches when staff have been trained.

All training should probably be done in two phases. Initial training should probably focus only on the philosophy of TQM, leaving the tools of TQM for a later time. Attempting to train middle managers and staff in both the philosophy and the tools of TQM at the same time is frequently too much for people and can bring about information overload.

Middle manager and staff training should include all the topics covered in this book, including the philosophy of TQM; the workings of quality teams; the collection and interpretation of customer quality data; and the use of process control charts, brainstorming, cause-and-effect diagrams, check sheets, and Pareto analysis. Additionally, middle management and staff training should also include the basics of sampling theory and the use of statistical analysis (e.g., correlation and regression analysis) in quality problem diagnosis and correction.

COLLECTING AND ANALYZING
CUSTOMER QUALITY DATA

Once all employees of a human service organization, or a division or unit, have been trained in the philosophy and tools of TQM, the next step is to begin collecting customer quality data. Focus groups can be used to gain initial insights into the quality dimension preferences of customers. Then, a system must be devised to regularly collect and analyze customer quality data.

FORMING QUALITY TEAMS

The regular analysis of customer quality data will identify areas where the organization is experiencing quality problems. The next step is to form quality teams and begin the real work of TQM: continuous quality improvement. Anyone, or any group in the organization, can propose the formation of a quality team and the selection of a quality problem to be worked on. All quality teams and quality problems identified must be approved by the quality council. This procedure is designed to ensure that quality teams are composed of the correct members and that they focus on important quality problems.

RECOGNIZING SUPERIOR QUALITY IMPROVEMENT

The quality council establishes incentives for significant quality improvements. In keeping with TQM's focus on teams and teamwork, group incentives rather than individual incentives are favored. Types of group incentives that can be used by a human service organization include cash awards, gain-sharing awards (where quality team members get to keep a portion of any cost savings achieved through their efforts), trips, release time, and various other forms of group recognition.

CONTINUOUS QUALITY IMPROVEMENT

Once a quality team has resolved a quality problem, it tackles another problem, or it disbands and the members join new quality teams. The process continues in its never ending quest for quality improvement.

AFTERWORD
Quality as a Journey

In Chapter 1, the reader was advised to remain skeptical about TQM, but asked not to judge until all the material in this book had been presented. That time has come. In the preceding pages, we have reviewed the history, the philosophy, and the tools of TQM. It is now time for the reader to decide if TQM is a relevant management system for human service organizations. I may be expressing a bias, but I think the reader will agree that it is.

What should be apparent to the reader at this point is that TQM is actually a relatively simple management system. Yes, TQM does have its own jargon, which can be troublesome at times. However, when we distill TQM down to its essence, what we find is a relatively simple philosophy of management with a set of relatively simple analytical tools. If one had to reduce TQM down to a single concept, "customer driven" might capture its essence as well as any. In TQM the customer is king, and the job of organizations is to make the king happy. This simple guiding principle brings a clarity of focus and an energy to the running of a human service organization—something that is frequently missing in other management systems.

What may be the most surprising thing about TQM is that the world took so long to discover it. Organizations have been run for just about every conceivable purpose. But only recently have we seriously considered running them for the benefit of customers.

One of the major advantages of TQM, of course, is its basic compatibility with human service and social work values. Human service professionals should find TQM philosophically harmonious with their own value system. Given TQM's widespread popularity, most human organizations will probably have a close encounter with it sometime during the decade of the 1990s. Given TQM's value base, the inevitable should perhaps be looked on more with anticipation than dread.

Finally, I would like to remind the reader that TQM is a journey, not a destination. TQM is not something you can do this year and forget about the year after. Continuous quality improvement is a never ending voyage of discovery.

REFERENCES

Albrecht, K. (1992). *The only thing that matters*. New York: Harper Business.

Alvesson, M., & Berg, P. (1992). *Corporate culture and organizational symbolism*. New York: Walter de Gruyter.

Barnard, C. (1938). *The functions of the executive*. Cambridge, MA: Harvard University Press.

Baruch, H. (1984). Structuring markets for public goods and services. In H. Brooks, H. Liebman, & C. Schelling (Eds.), *Public private partnerships: New opportunities for meeting social needs* (pp. 31-60). Cambridge, MA: Ballinger.

Benton, B., Field, T., & Millar, R. (1978). *Social services: Federal legislation vs. state implementation*. Washington, DC: The Urban Institute.

Brassard, M. (1988). *The memory jogger*. Methuen, MA: GOAL/QPC.

Brinkerhoff, R., & Dressler, D. (1990). *Productivity measurement*. Newbury Park, CA: Sage.

Business Week. (1991, October 25). The quality imperative. [Special issue].

Business Week. (1992, August 31). Management's new gurus, pp. 44-52.

Carr, D., & Littman, I. (1990). *Excellence in government—Total quality management in the 1990s*. Arlington, VA: Coopers & Lybrand.

Cohen, S., & Brand, R. (1990). Total quality management in the Environmental Protection Agency. *Public Productivity & Management Review, 14*, 99-114.

Crosby, P. (1980). *Quality is free*. New York: Mentor.

Crosby, P. (1985). *Quality without tears—The art of hassle-free management*. New York: Plume.

Crosby, P. (1992). *The eternally successful organization: The art of corporate wellness*. New York: Mentor.

Council of State Governments. (1983). *State & local government purchasing*. Lexington, KY: Author.

Deming, W. E. (1982). *Quality, productivity, and competitive position*. Cambridge: MIT Center for Advanced Engineering Study.

Deming, W. E. (1986). *Out of the crisis*. Cambridge: MIT Center for Advanced Engineering Study.

Deming, W. E. (1990). Transformation of American management. In K. Shelton (Ed.), *Empowering business resources*. Glenview, IL: Scott, Foresman.

Dobyns, L., & Crawford-Mason, C. (1991). *Quality or else*. Boston: Houghton-Mifflin.

Drucker, P. (1991). The new productivity challenge. *Harvard Business Review, 69*, 69-79.

Drucker, P. (1992). *Managing for the future*. New York: Truman Talley Books/Dutton.

Federal Quality Institute (FQI). (1991). *Introduction to total quality management in the federal government*. Washington, DC: Author.

Feigenbaum, A. (1983). *Total quality control* (3rd ed.). New York: McGraw-Hill.

Gabor, A. (1990). *The man who discovered quality*. New York: Times Books.

Garvin, D. (1991). How the Baldrige Award really works. *Harvard Business Review, 69*, 80-95.

George, W., & Gibson, B. (1991). Blueprinting—A tool for managing quality in service. In S. Brown, E. Gummesson, B. Edvardsson, & B. Gustavsson (Eds.), *Service quality*. Lexington, MA: Lexington Books.

Gitlow, H., Gitlow, S., Oppenheim, A., & Oppenheim, R. (1989). *Tools and methods for the improvement of quality*. Homewood, IL: Irwin.

Glenn, T. (1991). The formula for success in TQM. *The Bureaucrat, 20*, 17-20.

Goldense, R. A. (1991). Attaining TQM through employee involvement: Imperatives for implementation. *Journal of Management Science & Policy Analysis, 8*, 263-274.

Gummesson, E. (1991). Service quality: A holistic view. In S. Brown, E. Gummesson, B. Edvardsson, & B. Gustavsson (Eds.), *Service quality*. Lexington, MA: Lexington Books.

Hill, B., Blaser, C., & Balmer, P. (1986). Oversight and competition in profit vs. nonprofit contracts for home care. *Policy Studies Review, 5*, 588-597.

Hutchins, D. (1985). *Quality circles handbook*. New York: Nichols.

Imai, M. (1986). *Kaizen*. New York: Random House.

Ishikawa, K. (1985). *What is total quality control? The Japanese way* (D. Lu, Trans.). Englewood Cliffs, NJ: Prentice-Hall.

Jessome, P. (1988). The application of total quality control to a hospital setting. In R. Johnston (Ed.), *The management of service operations* (pp. 241-254). London: IFS.

Juran, J. (1988). *Juran's quality control handbook* (4th ed.). New York: McGraw-Hill.

Juran, J. (1989). *Juran on leadership for quality: An executive handbook*. New York: Free Press.

Kettle, D. F. (1988). *Government by proxy—(Mis?) managing federal programs*. Washington, DC: The Congressional Quarterly Press.

Kettner, P., & Martin, L. (1986). Making decisions about purchase of service contracting. *Public Welfare, 44*, 30-37.

Kettner, P., & Martin, L. (1987). *Purchase of service contracting*. Beverly Hills, CA: Sage.

Kettner, P., & Martin, L. (1993). Performance, accountability & purchase of service contracting. *Administration in Social Work, 17*.

Kettner, P., Moroney, L., & Martin, L. (1991). *Designing and managing programs*. Newbury Park, CA: Sage.

Koons, P. (1991). Getting comfortable with TQM. *The Bureaucrat, 20*, 35-38.

Krone, R. (1991). Symposium introduction total quality management TQM: Achievements, potentials, and pitfalls. *Journal of Management Science & Policy Analysis, 8*, 195-202.

Kronenberg, P., & Loeffler, R. (1991). Quality management theory: Historical context and future prospect. *Journal of Management Science & Policy Analysis, 8*, 203-221.

Kruger, R. (1988). *Focus groups: A practical guide for applied research*. Newbury Park, CA: Sage.

Lawler, E. (1990). *Strategic pay: Aligning organizational strategies and pay systems*. San Francisco: Jossey-Bass.

Lerner, A., & Wanat, J. (1992). *Public administration*. Englewood Cliffs, NJ: Prentice-Hall.

Maricopa County Department of Social Services. (1985). *Specialized transportation service (STS) ridership satisfaction survey no. 5*. Phoenix, AZ: Author.

Maricopa County Department of Social Services. (1991, January 2). *Vision, mission and values*. Phoenix, AZ: Author.

Maslow, A. (1962). *Toward a psychology of being*. Princeton, NJ: Van Nostrand.

Mayo, E. (1945). *The social problems of an industrial civilization*. Cambridge, MA: Harvard University Press.

Mesa Community College. (undated). *Total quality management*. Mesa, AZ: Author.

Milakovich, M. (1990). Total quality management for public sector productivity improvement. *Public Productivity & Management Review, 14*, 19-32.

Miller, T., & Miller, M. (1991). *Citizen surveys*. Washington, DC: International City Management Association.

Mills, P. (1990). On the quality of services in encounters: An agency perspective. *Journal of Business Research, 20*, 31-41.

Morgan, D. (1988). *Focus groups as qualitative research*. Newbury Park, CA: Sage.

Mossard, G. R. (1991). A TQM technical skills framework. *Journal of Management Science & Policy Analysis, 8*, 223-246.

Motorola. (1992). *Six sigma problem solving guide*. Plantation, FL: Author.

Mueller, C. (1980). Five years later—A look at title XX: The federal billion dollar social service fund. *Grantsmanship Center News, 8*, 27-37, 56-68.

Murdick, R., Render, B., & Russell, R. (1990). *Service operations management*. Boston: Allyn & Bacon.

Newsweek. (1992, March 16). Other people's money, pp. 46-47.

Osborn, D., & Gaebler, T. (1992). *Reinventing government*. Reading, MA: Addison-Wesley.

Patti, R. (1987). Managing for service effectiveness in social welfare: Toward a performance model. *Administration in Social Work, 11*, 7-22.

Perine, J. (1990). The quest for quality. *The Bureaucrat, 19*, 47-48.

Peters, T., & Austin, N. (1985). *A passion for excellence*. New York: Random House.

Peters, T., & Waterman, R. (1982). *In search of excellence*. New York: Warner Books.

Power, E. (1991). The differently enabled, organizations, and shame: Applications of qualitative TQM. *Journal of Management Science & Policy Analysis, 8*, 275-280.

Provost, L., & Norman, C. (1990). Variation through the ages. *Quality Progress, 23*, 39-44.

Pruger, R., & Miller, L. (1991a). Efficiency and the social services: Part A. *Administration in Social Work, 15*, 5-23.

Pruger, R., & Miller, L. (1991b). Efficiency and the social services: Part B. *Administration in Social Work, 15*, 25-44.

Rogers, R., & Hunter, J. (1992). A foundation of good management practice in government: Management by objectives. *Public Administration Review, 52*, 27-39.

Rosander, A. (1989). *The quest for quality in services*. White Plains, NY: American Society for Quality Control.

Saidel, J. (1991). Resource interdependency: The relationship between state agencies and nonprofit organizations. *Public Administration Review, 51*, 543-553.

Salamon, L. (1987). Of market failure, voluntary failure, and third-party government: Toward a theory of government-nonprofit relations in the modern welfare state. *Journal of Voluntary Action Research, 16*, 29-49.

Sheer, L. (1991). *Quality in higher education* [Monograph]. Lawrence: University of Kansas, School of Business.

Spendolini, M. (1992). *The benchmarking book*. New York: AMACON.

Strong, M., & Ford, B. (1992). Quality in state government: A grass-roots effort. *The Bureaucrat, 21*, 39-42.

Swiss, J. (1992). Adapting total quality management (TQM) to government. *Public Administration Review, 52*, 356-362.

Taylor, F. (1919). *The principles of scientific management*. New York: Harper & Brothers.

Terrell. P. (1987). Purchasing social services. *Encyclopedia of social work* (18th ed., pp. 434-442). Washington, DC: National Association of Social Workers.

Time. (1992, March 9). Charity begins at home, p. 48.

Wagenheim, G., & Reurink, J. (191). Customer service in public administration. *Public Administration Review, 51*, 263-270.

Walton, M. (1990). *Deming management at work*. New York: G. P. Putnam.

Watson, J., & Hopp, T. (1992, Winter). The private sector's experience with total quality management. *The GAO Journal*, 34-38.

Williams, H., & Webb, A. (1991). *Outcome funding—A new approach to public sector grantmaking*. Rensselaerville, NY: The Rensselaerville Institute.

Zeithaml, V., Parasuraman, A., & Berry, L. (1990). *Delivering quality services*. New York: Free Press.